The Pitch Coach

D1638762

First published in 2016 by
Liberties Press
140 Terenure Road North | Terenure | Dublin 6W
T: +353 (1) 405 5701| www.libertiespress.com | E: info@libertiespress.com

Trade enquiries to Gill & Macmillan Distribution
Hume Avenue | Park West | Dublin 12
T: +353 (1) 500 9534 | F: +353 (1) 500 9595 | E: sales@gillmacmillan.ie

Distributed in the United Kingdom by
Turnaround Publisher Services
Unit 3 | Olympia Trading Estate | Coburg Road | London N22 6TZ
T: +44 (0) 20 8829 3000 | E: orders@turnaround-uk.com

Distributed in the United States by
Casemate-IPM | 1950 Lawrence Road, Havertown, PA 19083
T: +1 (610) 853-9131 | E: casemate@casematepublishers.com

Copyright © Catherine Moonan, 2016
The author asserts her moral rights.

ISBN: 978-1-910742-24-2
2 4 6 8 10 9 7 5 3 1

A CIP record for this title is available from the British Library.

Internal design by Liberties Press
Cover design by Liberties Press

This book is sold subject to the condition that it shall not, by way of trade
or otherwise, be lent, resold, hired out or otherwise circulated, without the
publisher's prior consent, in any form other than that in which it is
published and without a similar condition including this condition
being imposed on the subsequent publisher.

No part of this publication may be reproduced or transmitted in any form
or by any means, electronic or mechanical, including photocopying, recording
or storage in any information or retrieval system, without the prior
permission of the publisher in writing.

The Pitch Coach

Your Guide to Presenting, Interviewing and Public Speaking

Catherine Moonan

This book is dedicated to the memory of my dear dad,
Tom Moonan (R.I.P., 1 December 2014),
who showed me that life is good and anything is possible.

Contents

Preface

Our deepest fear is not that we are inadequate.
Our deepest fear is that we are powerful beyond measure.
It is our Light, not our Darkness, that most frightens us.
We ask ourselves, who am I to be brilliant, gorgeous, talented, fabulous?
Actually, who are you not to be?
—Marianne Williamson, *A Return to Love*

Fear often holds us back and prevents us from doing or being what we are supposed to do or be. So what are we afraid of? Perhaps we have had a bad experience in the past, either in an interview, or during a time where we have had to speak in public. Perhaps it did not go as well as we would have liked. Well, that was then and this is now. We cannot change the past, but we can change our thinking around the now, which will determine the future. However, we have to start by believing we can change: to stop being afraid. By eliminating our fear, we are unstoppable. It would be such a shame to allow a fear of public speaking to prevent your light from shining to the world. Eliminate your fear, and the world will be a better place for it. It is your duty to yourself, the people around you and the world at large. Shine bright like a diamond.

Acknowledgements

I want to express my heartfelt thanks to each and every one of the industry experts who kindly contributed to *The Pitch Coach*. Their interviews provide wonderful insight into the art of pitching, presenting, interviewing and public speaking.

Thank you to Larry Bass, CEO of ShinAwiL, for his support in every way with this book. I am delighted to be part of series seven of 'Dragons' Den' in 2016. Thank you to Richard Curran, journalist and presenter of 'Dragons' Den' for writing the foreword. My thanks to the four former 'Dragons' Den' contestants for sharing their experience of pitching in the 'Den'; John Joyce, CTO at Yvolution; Siobhan King-Hughes, founder of Swift factory; Tara Dalrymple, founder of Feelsright; and Ollie Fegan, co-founder of usherU.

My thanks to Caitlin O'Connor, innovation strategist and networking expert; Eibhlin Curley, head of enterprise at Local Enterprise Office Dún Laoghaire Rathdown; John O'Sullivan, senior portfolio manager with Enterprise Ireland; Colm O'Maolmhuire, programme manager of the New Frontiers Programme in IT Tallaght; Wayne Murphy, CEO and programme director of Start Planet; Bill Liao, European Venture Partner with SOSventures and co-founder of CoderDojo; Eamonn Quinn, investment analyst and chairman at Kelsius;

Orla Rimmington, a partner with Kernel Capital; Seán O'Sullivan, managing director at SOSventures; George Zachary, general partner at Charles River Ventures; David Tighe, head of innovation at the Bank of Ireland; Brian Daly, programme manager at Techstars Berlin; Joshua Henderson, vice-president of Springboard Enterprises in Washington DC; Andy Shannon, Head of Startupbootcamp Global; Naomi Fein, founder of Think Visual; Joseph G. Lannig, sales director with Disney-ABC Television Group, New York; Orla Gallagher, HR specialist and executive coach at ESB; Brian Bowden, director of HR operations at Aer Lingus; Ken Cowley, recruitment consultant at Headhunt International; Garrett Taylor, fleet captain at Aer Lingus; Graeme Slattery, managing director at Notorious PSG; Simon Cocking, senior editor at *Irish Tech News*; Pamela Newenham, business journalist with the *Irish Times*; and Victoria Mary Clarke, author, broadcaster, journalist and media coach.

Thank you to Annie Birney and Bridget Sheerin, education officers at Glasnevin Cemetery Museum; Lawrence Bernstein, managing director at Great Speech Writing; Caroline Keeling, CEO at Keelings; Eamon Keane, CEO of Xpreso; James McElroy, co-founder of HouseMyDog; Gail Condon, founder of Writing For Tiny; Sinéad Kenny, CEO of DiaNia Technologies; Olive O'Connor, founder of MediStori; and Andrew MacFarlane, CEO of CareZapp.

My thanks to Peggy O'Regan, my former speech and drama teacher, and Sam Young, my meditation teacher, two inspirational people who helped to form the direction my career would take.

I am very grateful to my good friend, Catherine Gavin, for being my first official reader before I sent it to the publisher. My thanks to the publishing team at Liberties Press, particularly, Seán, Sam, Zoë and Karen.

A note of thanks to all my wonderful friends and family for their constant love and support, particularly my cousin Patricia from New York, and my good friends Edel and Mary, who helped me to plan, design and deliver my biggest 'Perfect Pitch' workshop to date, to 300 women in business as part of National Women's Enterprise Day 2013.

Thank you to my brother Seán and his wife Katrina, and to my mother-in-law, Patty. Finally, thanks to my mother, Carmel, whose prayers work miracles, to my husband, Gary, whose sense of humour also works miracles and to my three beautiful daughters, Alannah, Clíona and Ella, for being just the way they are.

Foreword

Richard Curran

Groucho Marx once said that a man who sounds well does well, but a man who looks well does better. If you want to pitch in the world of business, you have to give both your best shot.

Walking into the 'Dragons' Den' is not easy. I have always had admiration for those in any of the 500 or so pitches I have seen over the course of six series of the RTÉ television series. Some make it look easy. Some make it look difficult. But whether they are selling a wonderful business concept or something they dreamt up with a friend in the pub a few months earlier, it takes real guts to do.

'Dragons' Den' is both a slice of reality and a hugely popular television programme. The reality part of the show is that contestants are pitching genuine businesses to genuine investors, which may result in genuine deals.

It is how business works, yet it takes place in the most public of circumstances. Can you imagine walking into a job interview that you knew would be broadcast on national television?

I am always surprised by how many of those pitching in the 'Den' say they were nervous at the start of the pitch, but then became relaxed when the questions began.

The questions are the toughest and most gruelling part of the experience. So many people have a mental block when it comes to summarising, to an audience, something that they know inside out. They feel more confident about fielding gruelling questions for thirty minutes than summarising their business in two.

Naturally, some people are more nervous than others, but the good news is that many of the skills required to get that pitch right and provide the best possible chance of a good outcome can be learned.

Presenting has become a huge part of business, career and educational life. Many of us might think that we have never made a pitch in our lives. The truth is, we all pitch. If we have not pitched a business then we have still pitched ourselves, our skills and our employability many times. If you have ever looked for a bank loan, you have pitched. If you have ever been through a job interview, you have pitched.

In the world of business, pitching is becoming ever more common and ever more important. It involves everything from college-project presentations to winning a contract, from applying to a bank manager to securing a sizeable investment for your business. It might be delivering a talk at a conference, or being interviewed on radio or television. Yet those who are listening will make a judgement call about whether they would buy shares in your company, or even simply whether they would buy your product.

In a world with so many voices competing for attention, good pitching has had to change. It has to be succinct, clear and attention-grabbing, and it has to say something distinct about you. We all admire a good storyteller, someone who can be entertaining and engaging. A story well told draws us in, and often tells us something about who we are. By the same token, society values those who can communicate a message comprehensively, and with great attention to detail.

These used to be two very different skills – one engaging, the other authoritative. A good modern business pitch needs to do both, and in a relatively short period of time. Time constraints mean that the presenter has to make decisions about what facts are most important to their audience.

But do not worry. Many of these skills can be taught. While not everyone can write and deliver a Martin Luther King 'I Have a Dream' speech, you do have to deliver an impressive and professional business pitch.

Catherine Moonan's book, *The Pitch Coach* is a practical guide to understanding and delivering a solid pitch. It has been written by someone with enormous experience. She tailors the book to a variety of potential 'pitchers', and uses the insights of a range of interviewees to crystallise the key ingredients of a good pitch.

Among the many interviewees is Seán O'Sullivan of SOSventures, and formerly of 'Dragons' Den'. He is someone who has pitched to investors multiple times as he tried to secure backing for some of his early business ventures. He has also been pitched to hundreds of times.

Entrepreneurs like O'Sullivan provide great insight into what works and what does not work when compiling and delivering a pitch. Catherine also talks to venture capitalists and professional investors, some of whom see 300 pitches a year.

Readers of the book will get an understanding of what someone in that position is looking for in a pitch. You will also get a clear sense, as you pull your pitch together, of what works and what does not. What information should I include and what should I leave out? Should I make a joke? How should I stand, how should I sound and how should I look?

I have seen contestants go into 'Dragons' Den' and win over the 'Dragons' in the first sixty seconds. A great pitch alone will not land you the investment, but it gives you a great start. 'Dragons' on the show have often commented on how someone's pitch can leave them cold at the very start, which leaves the pitcher with an uphill battle.

One of the 'Dragons' said to me that choosing to invest in a business on the show was not easy because of the relatively small amount of time they have to digest what is being said before making a decision. He said it was like having somebody drive a car past you at thirty miles an hour, and having to decide, purely on that basis, whether or not you would buy it. Getting your pitch right is important as you may only have one chance to make the right impression, no matter what the circumstances.

Catherine Moonan draws on her own career path, and extensive experience in pitch training. She has delivered a practical and easy-to-read book which benefits everyone, from the start-up business person to the individual who wants to improve their presentation skills in work or in college.

Introduction

This book is designed to help anyone who would like to communicate their message more effectively when pitching, presenting, interviewing or speaking in public. You might be a start-up business pitching to a customer, client, supplier, business partner or investor. You might want to improve your presentations for work or college or you might have a formal speech to deliver at a corporate event. Perhaps you have an important interview coming up, or maybe you just have an interest in the content as it is not something you have ever thought about before. In this book, I share my own experience as a pitch coach, together with those from a myriad of industry experts. Whatever your reason for reading this book, I know you will get some valuable insight from the range of entrepreneurs, journalists, accelerator programme directors, corporate professionals and venture capitalists who have kindly given their time, and shared their unique knowledge and expertise in the art of pitching.

I have developed what I call the 'Perfect Pitch' workshop, based on coaching over 500 contestants on 'Dragons' Den' to date, in addition to the entrepreneur and corporate training that I have also been doing for a number of years. I have found that people tend to overcomplicate and over intellectualise their pitch or presentation. As a result, some people make life more difficult for themselves, and increase the stress often associated with public speaking. If they follow the steps in this workshop, I believe it will help to clarify the message they want to communicate. After all, if they are not clear in their own mind about the message they want to communicate, how can they expect the audience to understand the message clearly?

I initially developed the workshop to help start-ups to design and deliver their investment pitches. I was asked to develop a workshop for thirty people at UCD's Innovation Academy. I had been thinking of trying out a new technique for a while. As the Innovation Academy promoted creativity, I asked if I could incorporate mindful breathing meditation, music and colour into my workshop. The programme managers were happy for me to try it out. It worked beautifully. By the end of the workshop, everyone in the room was able to stand up in front of the group and deliver a sixty-second pitch.

I quickly realised that I could use the same workshop to help corporates with their business presentations. I have used it myself to develop a clearer vision for what I wanted to deliver in this book.

The objective of the workshop is to provide people with the framework for their pitch, presentation or speech. Their actual pitch, presentation or speech may well be five, ten or twenty minutes long, but this framework will help to clarify their message, and they can then expand on the various points they wish to make. Consider the sixty-second pitch as an executive summary. Imagine someone missed your pitch or presentation and then bumped into you afterwards, maybe in the elevator, and said, 'Sorry I missed your talk earlier. I heard it was great – what was it about?' You do not have those five, ten or twenty minutes to re-cap on everything, but you do have sixty seconds. It is amazing what information you can get across in sixty seconds.

I have outlined that workshop in this book. The fact that you are not limited to any workshop time frame means that you can spend as much or as little time on it as you want. I once managed to deliver this workshop to 300 business women in one hour and fifteen minutes, as part of a networking event for National Women's Enterprise Day 2013. By the end of it, 300 women were able to deliver a sixty-second pitch about their business. I have delivered it to many senior managers and directors at the corporate level, as well as to start-up and accelerator programmes all over Ireland and the UK. I have also delivered the workshop at Women in Business and Chamber of Commerce networking events, as well as to the national finalists of the Ireland's Best Young Entrepreneur competition in 2014 and 2015. You can do it in less than an hour. Just work with whatever time frame you have. Try it. It's simple, but it works.

Chapter One

LIFE'S A PITCH

We are constantly pitching our ideas, ourselves, our points of view. However, pitching is an art, not a science, and it is certainly not rocket science – there is no exact formula.

Like all art forms, you can start by understanding what techniques increase the chance of a positive outcome. After this, it comes down to practising the delivery of your pitch, then reviewing your pitch and going back to the drawing board, taking what you have learned, and working towards a better pitch next time. Pitching is a learning-by-doing process; the more often you do it, the better you become. Pitching is also personal. No two pitches are the same, nor should they be. Your pitch is ever-evolving. The pitch you deliver today will be different to the one you deliver next week and next month. Your pitch will change depending on changes in your team or your product, new clients, receiving investment. The best way to think of your pitch is as a story. It is your unique story. Your story is ever-changing, and so is your pitch. There are still certain elements to your story that need to be there, particularly for an investor. We will go into that in more detail later on. Ultimately, though, the way in which you tell your story is very important. Regardless of how technical your idea, product or service is, your story must be simple and engaging. It must be made real and tangible to anyone listening: a) they must be able to understand what you are talking about, and b) you have to engage them. If your pitch has done both of these things, you have made it memorable – you have, by doing this, made it easy for your audience to remember your idea, product or service, and to be able to tell someone else about it.

Your pitch should be from the heart as well as the head. You need to find that emotional connection between you and the audience by bringing in the human element, and making your audience care. It is not just about facts, figures and statistics – you need to make your pitch relevant to your audience. It is not a one-size-fits-all, but needs to change depending on the audience. Your pitch to an investor, for example, will be different from a pitch to a customer, client, supplier or business partner.

I use the name 'Perfect Pitch' for my workshop, but what is perfect? Is there any such thing? Facebook uses the slogan 'Done is better than perfect', which I think is brilliant. I have borrowed it here. Quite often, as you may well know, we put off showing something because it is not perfect. We are afraid to pitch our idea, because we feel that it is not quite there yet. Well, remember: 'Done is better than perfect'. Take the leap. I like to combine that slogan with the Nike slogan 'Just do it'. Practise makes perfect, and you learn by doing.

Glossophobia

I had often heard of a fear of public speaking, but I never realised that it affected so many people. It is called 'glossophobia'. Research carried out in the US claims that it is people's number-one fear. Studying speech and drama from the age of five, until I earned my teaching diploma helped me to build my self-confidence by regularly having to recite poetry and prose in front of exam adjudicators, and even acting out excerpts from plays. Taking part in a school play or musical can really help children to overcome any fear of public speaking – or 'performance anxiety' – from a young age. Debating in school is also a great way to develop public-speaking skills. However, many students leave school having never taken part in a school play or debating team and, as a result, it comes as a shock to the system when they must stand up and speak in front of a group of people. I have met several people through my training and coaching who strongly dislike any form of public speaking. For some, their dislike is as a result of a bad experience. One very successful businesswoman I spoke with said that her first presentation ever was in her first year in college. It went so badly for her that she was thirty-five before she did another one, and that was only because she had to. Even an interview situation can prove to be quite challenging for some people.

I use the expression 'shock to the system' because that is what it can feel like. I worked with a manager once who could not thank his staff at the Christmas party without the sweat dripping from his brow and his hands shaking. He was more than competent in his fields of finance and IT, yet something as simple as standing up and saying thank you to his colleagues incapacitated him.

Public speaking can do that to people. It is called the fight-or-flight response, and it is an automatic, physical response, designed to help us take rapid action when we feel that we are under threat. Of course, public speaking does not pose a physical threat. If anything, it is an emotional threat, but the brain does not seem to be able to distinguish between the two.

When thinking about setting up my own business, I recalled that manager and his struggle with public speaking. I knew there must be others like him. I also realised that this could be perceived as something negative. 'Well, if he cannot stand up and present his ideas clearly, is he also incompetent at his job?' Not at all. However, effective communication and presentation skills are essential not just for managers, but for all employees within an organisation. Effective communication is a life skill.

We all need to be able to stand up and speak clearly about the message we want to share with others. It may be a pitch, presentation, interview or speech. It may be advocating for a sick child or an elderly parent who cannot speak for themselves. In either case, this is not the time to be shy. It does not serve you well. The world needs to hear your message, loud and clear.

I decided to combine my experience as a manager in Compaq Computers with my previous experience as a French and German secondary-school teacher, and set up Communication Matters in September 2002. I sent out sixty letters to various organisations at the time, and received one response, from the Bank of Scotland (Ireland). After several meetings with the communications manager, he booked me for three dates that November to deliver training in effective communication and presentation skills to their senior managers and directors from

Ireland and the UK. I think it was my speech and drama experience that won him over. They hired the Carolan Room in the National Concert Hall, which, I was told, they use for the President. I hired a video-production company for the day so that each participant would get a copy of their own presentation on video. I had never done this before. I had eight weeks to prepare for this training. Was I worried? I was terrified.

Call to Journalism

All you need is one good recommendation or testimonial, and you are in business. Thankfully, I got that with the Bank of Scotland (Ireland), and I followed it with trainings and testimonials from An Post and BUPA Ireland. In addition to delivering training in presentation skills to corporates, I also started teaching a pitching module on the Dublin Institute of Technology's Hothouse Programme for Entrepreneurs. Then, in 2007, I decided to apply for the MA in Journalism in Dublin City University. It was my third attempt. I had applied twice when I first left college in the early 1990s. When I was not accepted, I ended up doing the Higher Diploma in Education in Trinity College, Dublin, which qualified me as a French and German teacher.

My interest in journalism had always been niggling in the background. Seventeen years later, after reading *The Right to Write* and *The Artist's Way*, both by Julia Cameron, and doing a course on *The Artist's Way* with a wonderful man called Sam Young, I applied a third time to do the MA in Journalism. It is all about timing. This time, I was accepted. As part of the application process, I had to have had something published. By chance, I had written my very first article earlier that year, about confidence-building for women returning to work after years being at home with the kids. That morning, I had heard a caller on 'The Gerry Ryan Show', a woman who had spent nine years at home taking care of her children, and was now returning to work outside of the home. She was very anxious. The discussion that ensued between Gerry Ryan and that lady inspired me to write the piece, which I sent to the *Irish*

Independent's 'Mothers and Babies' section. It was published, and I received a cheque for €200.

When I was finally accepted onto the full-time MA in June of that year, I had my own business, and was married with three young children. No pressure. I loved the course, and the highlight for me was a work placement as a researcher in RTÉ's 'Prime Time' after a gruelling interview process. My dissertation was a forty-minute radio documentary, 'Angels'. I subsequently pitched it to a television production company, and we produced a seven-minute television piece on 'Angels' which aired on RTÉ's 'Capital D' in June 2009. Meanwhile, I had pitched an article to the *Irish Independent* 'Health and Living' supplement about going back to college full-time with three young children. They published it, along with over twenty more feature articles in the next five years.

In 2014 I started working on a community radio station, Dublin City FM, where I reviewed the papers and had two interviews on 'Good Morning Dublin' on Thursday mornings. One of my interviews ended up being with an old classmate from the MA, Pamela Newenham, the *Irish Times* business journalist. She had contacted me about her new book, *Silicon Docks*, which I read before the radio interview and loved. A few days later, I was sitting in my kitchen admiring every aspect of the book – the cover, the font, the paper – and looked to see who the publisher was: Liberties Press. I looked up their website and sent them an e-mail, pitching a book on pitching. They replied the next day requesting a meeting. We met, and the end result is in your hands. Literally.

Introduction to Start-ups

I continued with my small training business while back in college between 2007 and 2008. It was my second year teaching the module for DIT's Hothouse, titled 'Preparing and Perfecting Your Pitch'. My friend Catherine Gavin was working in California at the time, and she sent me a short video clip of the inaugural 'Entrepreneur Idol', which had just taken place in Stanford University. It was a take-off from the Fox TV show 'American Idol'. The video showed three finalists out of the sixty MBA students, pitching their best business idea in sixty seconds to a panel of four: Matt Marshall, founder of Venture Beat, and three venture capitalists (VCs) from Charles River Ventures. The idea for 'Entrepreneur Idol' came from George Zachary, one of the VCs on the panel. Charles River Ventures had sponsored the event in order to embed its name in future business leaders. After all, previous students of Stanford Business School had gone on to set up Google Inc. The winner would get $2000 in seed money. The video also showed panel feedback, feedback that was not just based on the idea, or financial analysis, or market research. In fact, some of the students had just come up with the idea the previous day. The feedback was, for the most part, focused on how the pitch was delivered. The panel spoke about the use of props, and of grabbing attention at the start by opening with a bold claim. They spoke about having variation within your voice, about body language and displaying passion for what you were talking about. I was fascinated by this video, and showed it to the group of entrepreneurs in DIT. I decided to incorporate the sixty-second pitch as part of their training, in addition to five- and ten-minute pitches. Some of the start-ups later came back to me and said that the sixty-second pitch had been the most beneficial, the one that they used time and time again.

I found that I really enjoyed working with start-ups. The environment provided a very different dynamic to working in the corporate world, and the energy and enthusiasm had a ripple effect. One of the programme's participants, Niall Harbison, went over to the UK 'Dragons' Den' and secured a £50,000 investment for his business Simply Zesty. Niall was very confident at telling his story, and I knew that not everyone would be able to do that. I had not even heard of 'Dragons' Den' prior to working with DIT's Hothouse. Little did I know then that, not only would I hear a great deal more about 'Dragons' Den', but I would actually start working with the Irish version of the programme.

My Pitch to 'Dragons' Den'

In an article in the *Sunday Business Post* in September 2008, I read that the production company ShinAwiL was bringing the TV show 'Dragons' Den' to Irish television screens on RTÉ. My immediate thought was, 'Irish people are really going to struggle with this two-minute pitch'. I decided to contact ShinAwiL. In reality, I pitched myself to 'Dragons' Den'. I sent an e-mail, but received no response. I followed up with a phone call a few days later. They had not received my mail (it had gone to junk mail) and they asked me to resend it. I explained on the phone that I wanted to work with the programme as a presentation coach. In addition to helping people to overcome their nerves and present effectively, I felt that I could help people tell their story. Initially, over the phone, they said 'no', and that they did not need a presentation coach. 'Dragons' Den' was a franchise and in eighteen different countries. They already had a list of people required for their production team, and there was no spot for a 'presentation coach' on that list. I said that was fine, but that they still may want to have a think about it. I resent the mail anyway.

At that stage I had worked with many people on their presentations. I knew how nervous people got, and that was without the additional pressure of television cameras and 'Dragons'. I received a phone call from ShinAwiL a few weeks before filming. They asked me to come in for a meeting. I was not a bit nervous – they had already said 'no' over the phone, so I had nothing to lose. As far as I was concerned, it was just a chat. I met with Larry Bass, CEO of ShinAwiL, and Eugenia Cooney, the original series producer of 'Dragons' Den'. We chatted about my training in presentation skills with both corporates and start-ups, my MA in Journalism and my internship in RTÉ 'Prime Time'. We agreed to trial my presentation coaching, for the first year, and see how it went. I was delighted. I have worked with ShinAwiL on 'Dragons' Den' every year since and have loved every minute of it. During series one, I became known among contestants and the ShinAwiL team as the 'pitch coach'. That name has stuck with me since then. I have coached over 500 contestants over the six series to date, and helped them to gain over €4 million in investment. I am looking forward to working on series seven of 'Dragons' Den', in 2016.

Angels in Their Pockets

Nerves, going blank, speaking too fast and information overload are just some of the many issues facing the contestants waiting to enter the 'Dragons' Den'. For the majority of entrants, this is a once-in-a-lifetime opportunity. Many never dreamed of being on television, and possibly never will be again. This is their chance to shine. They have come up with a unique product or service which they believe in wholeheartedly. All they have to do then is deliver a two-minute pitch to convince one or more of the five 'Dragons' that their idea is worth investing in.

It sounds fairly straightforward. Even easy, perhaps. Two minutes is not a particularly long time. What could possibly go wrong? Let's see . . . where will I start? You could forget the name of your business. You could even forget your own name. You could forget to ask the 'Dragons' for investment. You could become so consumed by a fear of public speaking that no words come out at all. It is a huge relief to many participants that they have an opportunity to go over their pitch before facing the 'Dragons', regardless of how competent they felt they were with public speaking. We had a lot of pacing up and down, looking through notes, delivering the pitch, making changes, repeating the pitch, stopping, starting, stopping, pitching one more time, once more, and again, and one last time . . . There comes a point where there is no more time, as the 'Dragons' are waiting in their 'Den'.

As a pitch coach I find that, first and foremost, I have to calm people down, to ground them, talk to them, listen to their fears and focus them. I have to get them to forget about themselves and what people might think of them. To forget worrying about making mistakes, and concentrate on getting their message across to the audience – the 'Dragons', in this case. I try to convince them that their product is unique, that they are unique and that this is a wonderful opportunity to show off their idea to the 'Dragons'. Nobody knows their idea better than them. For some people I use techniques such as positive affirmation, visualisation and simple breathing exercises. People need to trust that the right words will come out.

I advise against learning the lines of a pitch off by heart. If you get fixated on a certain way of saying something, you increase your chance of going blank in the event that you lose your train of thought. I find that if you follow a logical structure, with a few keywords in your head to guide you, the rest of the words will flow freely. It also sounds more natural than learning lines. The content of any pitch or presentation should be based on the audience. In this case, why are the 'Dragons' here? What do they want to know? What do they need to know? What interests them? You cannot expect them to be interested just because you are standing in front of them. You have to work at making your pitch interesting. You need to give them a taste of your idea so that when you are finished, they will want to know more.

Do not forget that the 'Dragons' are themselves entrepreneurs, and that they want to make money. Entice them. You need to have a clear objective about what you want to leave the 'Den' with: investment.

How you deliver your pitch is crucial. You need to come across as confident for others to be confident in you and your idea. The actual delivery of your pitch can have much more of an impact than the content itself. Perfecting your pitch is about having the correct posture, projecting your voice, pronouncing your words clearly and varying your voice within sentences. It is about emphasising important words, not being afraid to pause and not dropping your voice at the end of sentences. It is about making it more interesting for your audience by connecting with them, using eye contact and gestures that reinforce your message.

The old saying of 'practice makes perfect' is never truer than in pitches, presentations or any type of public speaking. An entrepreneurial pitch for investment is like a stage performance. You need the audience to believe in you. The role you are playing is yourself, but the best version of yourself. In a two-minute pitch, you need to step out of your comfort zone, forget your inhibitions and let yourself and your idea shine.

I mentioned people's fear of public speaking. I have seen this fear first-hand. I have met 'Dragons' Den' contestants with angels in their pockets, crystals in their hands and memorial cards of loved ones who have died inside their jacket pockets. One lady had a personal healer with her, playing soft music and fanning her down beforehand.

When I meet contestants for the first time and ask them to run through their pitch, some people just go blank, and cannot even remember their name. This can happen after sleepless nights spent thinking and worrying about their pitch. I know if there had not been someone there beforehand, listening to their pitch over and over, encouraging them, breaking it down into keywords for them, some contestants would have bolted out the door beforehand. I would invest in every single one of them for getting up off the couch, putting themselves forward and undergoing the harrowing ordeal that is pitching on 'Dragons' Den'.

Chapter Two

PITCHING 'DRAGONS' DEN' TO RTÉ

'Dragons' Den' – or 'Shark Tank' as it is called in the US and Australia – is a television programme that allows several entrepreneurs an opportunity to present their varying business ideas to a panel of five wealthy investors, and pitch for financial investment, offering a stake of the company in return. The format of the programme is owned by Sony Pictures, and is based on the original Japanese series sold worldwide. On the last count, eighteen countries had their own versions of 'Dragons' Den'. The programme has been produced by ShinAwiL for RTÉ television since its inception, and was first broadcast for RTÉ in April 2009.

Interview with Larry Bass, CEO of ShinAwiL – the Man Behind the Irish 'Dragons'

Can you tell us about ShinAwiL?

ShinAwiL has a reputation for being a production company that produces various international formats. We are best known for the Irish versions of 'The Voice of Ireland', 'Masterchef', 'The Apprentice', 'Dragons' Den', 'You're a Star', 'Charity You're a Star' and 'Popstars'. The most recent show is 'Home of the Year'. At the time when 'Dragons' Den' became the show that it is, we had already produced a number of other international shows, and I was a fan of the show. I thought that it was a really clever way of bringing business onto television, and adding drama. I spoke to the rights holders, Sony, and negotiated a deal for the Irish rights.

How did you go about pitching 'Dragons' Den' to RTÉ?

My initial pitch to RTÉ was not very good as they did not go for it, their reasons being the cost and the fact that it was not original. I then came up with the idea of partnering with a financial institution. Pitching to get 'Dragons' Den' on air was a war of attrition, rather than a single pitch. It was a series of conversations, a three-year journey to getting the show on air. The most appropriate attribute was persistence. Not taking 'no' for an answer. You need to keep going back, but also have self-preservation. Find a different route, find a different door. After three years of that, it became a very solid proposal.

How important is persistence?

In our business we pitch hundreds of times a year and only make four or five programmes. You always learn from whatever experience you have. You have to keep moving forward, because if you allow a knockback or a 'no' to stop you, you will never be in business.

What background research did you have to do?

When we eventually got the green light from RTÉ and began on pre-production, the original series producer, Eugenia Cooney, and myself went over and visited a recording of the 'Dragons' Den' in the UK. I do not think it taught us anything that we did not know, but it was interesting to talk to the UK 'Dragons' – to get their feeling for why they were doing the show and what they were getting out of it, so that we could have the same conversations with people we wanted to cast for the Irish 'Dragons'. It is important to tell people that if they do this, they are exposing themselves. It is their own money that they are going to have to invest. We also wanted to benefit from the wisdom of people who had done this before.

Why do you think 'Dragons' Den' works as a television programme?

The reason 'Dragons' Den' works is because it is natural human drama. Nobody is given lines. What you see is absolutely real. Yes, we edit, but we do not give anyone a script. We do not give second chances.

How important is the story?

Having sat through a fair portion of the pitches on 'Dragons' Den' and other shows, and having participated in pitches and pitching other broadcasters, one of the most important things is the story. People buy off people. People connect with people through story. For me, it does not matter what you are selling or what you are pitching, or what you are trying to achieve. If you cannot connect the person you are talking to with a story they can have some type of connection to, they are not building any sort of bridge between what you are doing and what they may or may not want to do with you. The story for me is the heart of the pitch. Why are we here? Where is it taking us? What am I going to get? How is it relevant? I try and bring in real life, and actually make a connection with the people I am talking to. It is hugely important that they actually believe what you are saying. It is important that they have a sense of belief in you, because you are the person who has to deliver it.

How is the Irish version of 'Dragons' Den' different from other versions of the programme?

Storytelling is one of the things that makes the Irish version of 'Dragons' Den' uniquely different to other versions around the world. We are a land of natural storytellers. It is in our DNA. Not only do we have a great storytelling capacity as individuals, the 'Dragons' have the capacity to hear stories, engage with them and go off on tangents. That is who we are. We have a culture of meeting in the pub or meeting in the church. People in Ireland talk. We solve life's problems by having a conversation over a cup of tea. That is part of who we are. In other cultures they do not talk like that. They certainly do not do it in the same way that we do.

Why do people overcomplicate a pitch?

A pitch becomes complicated, number one, when you let it, and number two, when people rate the importance of the moment too highly. Everywhere I go, I am pitching. It might be to a sponsor, broadcaster or someone I want to take part in the show. I will spend a whole day preparing for two pitches I have later in the week, even though I have been doing it all day, every day, for twenty years. Preparation is key, as is not allowing the importance of what we are doing later in the week to take over and block it. It is just another pitch. Our ability to be successful is based on our ability to be natural, and give people what they want.

How do you prepare for a pitch?

Every pitch is different. There are always different elements that you are trying to go in and answer. I do a lot of cold-calling, so, going into the marketing department of a corporate company, maybe trying to get them to sponsor a TV show. At first they are just obliging me by having a meeting. There is a sense of intrigue. They are meeting us, so, to some degree, they are obviously interested. Then I try to pre-empt, and suggest why they should engage with us. To have the correct story, you need to know some background. We try to go in and have a 'listening meeting' first. We came up with the concept of a 'listening meeting' in order to have a more successful conversation – a more successful story. If we went in and said, 'Right, one size fits all', it does not work. It gives them the benefit of input. It means they have got ownership of what you are talking to them about. What do they want? What does their brand do? Who do they talk to? What would they like? What would be a win for them? What would be a bonus? Then we take all that and we go away, and try to construct the right pitch or proposal. So if we were doing something from a television point of view that talked to that brand, what does it look like? We then try to construct a proposal based on what the client wants.

Going into any pitch without adequate preparation is a big mistake. You have to know who you are talking to. You have to know their track record in decision making in the area at hand. You need to have the ability, if nothing else, to remark on something that they have done before.

How important is the team?

One of the key things for us is the team. The team is always incredibly important. I think that is one of the things we lean on, because our track record is there. It is something that we earned. It is like respect – you cannot go out and buy it, you have to build it. That track record is incredibly important to us. Included in that track record is the fact that we are not the cheapest company in the world to work with. We have lost pitches on price. But you pay for what you get. We never compromise on quality. Once we start compromising on that, we are no longer ShinAwiL. When pitching you still need to be true to your values – who you are and what you stand for, and how you build that DNA into what you are pitching – whether it is a product or a service. People have to believe it. I keep going back to the simple principle of the story. The story has to include all these elements.

How would you describe pitching?

I use the analogy of learning to drive. Pitching is like when you learn to drive a car – you have to use the handbrake correctly, look in the mirror, indicate and then drive off. After you are driving for a year or two, it becomes automatic.

There are many things you need to learn when you are learning to drive. It is the same with pitching. There are many things you learn in order to be present, to physically be there in the room with your audience. They are the elements that you pick up along the way. Some of them will not be there initially, and you will learn from bitter experience – 'Oh, if only we had done whatever . . . ' Well, you will do that the next time.

How important is it to be 'in the moment' when pitching?

For really important pitches, one of the things I have learned is that it is really important to have a sole focus, that you are not easily distracted. I have the attention span of a goldfish, but when I am in a really important pitch, nothing distracts me. You have got to be there, and that is a very difficult thing for people, especially entrepreneurs.

I had to do a pitch recently in an international environment. It was a pitch competition, and I had the benefit of watching eleven other companies pitch before me. This is an interesting thing, which I had never done before. We prepared a little mood reel and a PowerPoint presentation, and I had asked a couple of the key talent to come with me to the pitch. So: we're in Paris, we're in the location, we're in a room with an audience who have seen two hours of presentations before our pitch. People were losing the will to live in that room, so I threw the whole pitch out the window. Instead of going through the PowerPoint presentation we had prepped, I played the mood reel and then just let people read the PowerPoint. I interviewed the two talent without doing a presentation. The one thing I noticed was that there was no Q&A with any other pitch, whereas a lot of people were engaging with us, and walking up and reading our slides. We were pitching for a TV drama. It was to financiers, broadcasters and distributors – people who could provide finance. The other people in the room pitching would describe what the drama was and what genre it fell into, and would then literally read out the information with their heads down. Jim Sheridan, who was with me as our director, taught me that books and reading are 'face-down', and film is 'face-out'. Pitching is also 'face-out' – it is about connecting. The decision to drop the slides was made while walking up to do the presentation.

When you have a great storyteller like Jim Sheridan in the room, you don't waste it. So, read the room.

Do you ever get nervous when pitching?

Sometimes my nerves manifest themselves after the pitch, when waiting to hear back about a decision. This does not go away. Nerves might also manifest themselves when you are about to do the first production.

When pitching, you can find yourself thrown through no fault of your own. You arrive in a room and the people you expected might be somewhat different – you do not have total control over who may be in the room. So I always ask the question 'Who are we pitching to?' You do not want a passenger there that you feel you are not talking to, because you do not know what they are there for and that can throw people easily. Or, someone could just be having a bad day, and they are sitting there opposite you in that room and it does not really matter what you are going to say. Sometimes it just is not going to work. Or, you might have something, but the fit is just not right. It goes back to not allowing 'nos' to determine who you are, or what you do next. It is never personal. It is just business.

What makes the drama so good on 'Dragons' Den'?

We make a big thing of people walking up the stairs on 'Dragons' Den'. They are walking into a theatre, they have left everything in their life behind. They are going on a journey. As human beings, we are conditioned to want to follow journeys. All stories have a 'once upon a time' and then a 'happy ending' or not. That is the way we are conditioned, that is our human instinct. In every pitch, you need to have that beginning, middle and end. If you do not have that, it will not work. I think the best drama is the kind that unfolds in a natural way, where people have to walk up the stairs and into that room, they have no idea what is going to happen, they have not had a rehearsal. They are living on their wits. It is absolutely amazing. It is a credit to you, Catherine, how few of them come up and can't deliver. It does not really happen. It is funny how there is that natural fight-or-flight instinct that we have. It takes over. Most of the people who come in must be a bundle of nerves, because it is the most unnatural thing they are probably ever going to do. How many times in your life are you going to walk in and pitch something on national television? When people do it I am always immensely proud that they have hit the mark and delivered, and I am always surprised at how well they deliver, considering how unnatural and how unnerving it is. But if people know their brief, if they know their product and they know it inside out, they quickly start to get into a comfort zone. If you have got knowledge of what you are talking about, you can be consistent, powerful and believable. And that is key. It is very important that salient facts are part of what you are doing.

Chapter Three

PITCHING: WHERE DO YOU START?

Tailoring Your Pitch
to Your Target Audience

The starting point of any pitch is the audience. Who are you pitching to? It might be to an investor, or it might be to a potential customer, client, supplier or business partner. You need to know your business more than anyone, and you need know who you will be pitching to. You must remember that every audience is different, find out what they are looking for and give it to them on a silver platter. The content of your pitch will change depending on the audience. If you are presenting the same message to a different audience, maybe eighty-five percent of your content will be the same, but examples, anecdotes or case studies will need to be tweaked for each individual audience.

There are a few things you need to remember about any audience.

They need to be convinced. Do not think that because you are standing up in front of a group of people they will listen to you or be interested in what you have to say. I used to be a French and

German secondary-school teacher, so I learned this lesson early on in my career. When it comes to your audience, it is your job to engage and entertain them from the start, right the way through your pitch.

You are not going to be able to give all the information you would like to give in a designated space of time. You need to be selective. You are far better off leaving the audience wanting more than boring them with so much information that they cannot wait for you to sit down.

Simplify your topic. Do not overcomplicate or over-intellectualise it – you need to be as inclusive as possible towards your audience. You do not want to alienate them in any way, by using technical words or jargon they do not understand. With an international audience, be careful to avoid slang, idioms or metaphors that they may not understand. If they are confused about a word or a phrase you just said ten seconds ago, they are not listening to what you are saying right now.

In an interview with singer-songwriter Glen Hansard and his band, The Frames, in the July 2015 issue of *CARA*, the Aer Lingus in-flight magazine, Glen's band member Colm Mac Com Iomaire said:

> We have a unique relationship with our audience in that we realise they are integral to the sort of performances we deliver – and that goes back to us as buskers making music on the street. From moment to moment, street musicians have very strong antennae, and Glen is brilliant at reading an audience; he has a sense of being able to keep everyone with you and to take off in tangents, or to stop and turn at any point.

Glen interjected:

> While gigs can turn this way or that on the flick of a coin, they are essentially about empathy. It's looking into a room full of people and sensing that it needs something, some song – something to kick off the night. That definitely comes from busking and being able to read the mood. Whenever we use the heart, pretty much everything goes great.

Do not be afraid to speak from the heart as well as the head. When you speak from the heart, you connect with people. Think of all the sayings associated with the heart – 'That was a half-hearted attempt', 'Her heart was low', 'No heart', 'Cold heart', 'My heart is broken', 'A change of heart', 'Bleeding-heart', 'Heart full of gold', 'My heart wasn't in it', 'Absence makes the heart grow fonder'. If you genuinely want to connect with people, it is the only real way. Cross my heart.

If possible, research your audience in advance. I have drafted a sample audience questionnaire in chapter eight of this book. In the meantime, you can start thinking about who you will be pitching to.

1. Who is in your audience? Are they male or female? What age group does your audience comprise of? Are they middle-aged male and female colleagues, venture capitalists or chefs? Is there a mix of people in the audience? If possible, list them out. If you do not know, make some calls and try to find out. Keep this in mind when using examples in your pitch, presentation or speech. On one occasion when attending an awards ceremony for technical start-ups, I was taken aback by the sexist example used by the master of ceremonies at the event. I believe he thought he was talking to an all-male

audience. Whatever about alienating your audience, it was downright rude to insult them.

2. What are their roles, responsibilities and interests? By researching your audience, it might help you to choose the right examples, case studies or anecdotes for your pitch, presentation or speech. I once coached a lady who was pitching a community project, and wanted a partnership deal with another organisation. When researching the audience, she found out that one of the panel members had a passion for swimming and had won many swimming events. So, to capture her attention, she used an opening slide of a black-and-white photograph of hundreds of people wearing old swimming costumes and swimming caps diving into a river from both sides. The image of course captivated the audience, and she went on to negotiate her plan for the community project.

3. How will your audience benefit from hearing what you have to say? What is in it for them? Why should your audience care about what you have to say? You need to imagine them sitting in front of you saying, 'So what? Why should I care?' Are you going to help them to save time or money, for example? Everyone's time is precious. You are taking up their time with this pitch, presentation or speech. Making your pitch relevant to your audience can help to validate your use of their time. For example, you might be pitching a product that helps in the detection of breast cancer. Your audience consists of medics and venture capitalists, and both are interested for different reasons: the medics want to save the patient and the venture capitalists want a return on investment.

4. What do they already know about your topic? Do they know more or less than you? Be mindful of this. Where knowledge is concerned, you have to play to the lowest common denominator. In a medical presentation to a large audience, for example, that includes venture capitalists who are not medical experts, you might say something like this: 'For those of you who don't know, CSF means cerebrospinal fluid. I will be calling it CSF from now on.'

5. What are the three things this audience needs to know about you? What is going to impress them? Is it important that they know that you are the founder of the company? Should you tell them about your twenty years of experience in IT? Would it be helpful if they knew that you have already received an award for your idea, product or service?

6. How can you emotionally connect with your audience? You should try to find an emotional connection with your audience. I know it is not always possible, but if you are mindful of it, you might get an opportunity at the end, if you have a period for questions and answers. Our psyches are made up of logic and emotion, and you need to tap into the emotions of an audience, and capture their hearts as well as their minds. If we are talking about a cure for breast cancer, for example, you need to bring in the human element. It is more than likely that everyone in the audience has been affected by cancer, either directly or indirectly. Get them to empathise.

7. What do you want your audience to do, think or feel as a result of what you are going to say? Have a clear objective about why you are speaking in the first place. Do you want to convince or persuade your audience to do something?

Do you want them to think a little differently about a particular cause? Do you want them to feel inspired as a result of what you have to say?

8. What questions do you think your audience might ask? Make a list of questions or objections they may have. Troubleshoot them with a friend or colleague beforehand. You may not anticipate everything, but having some preparation done will increase your confidence when it comes to questions or objections. You should think about including any obvious questions in the pitch, presentation or speech. Otherwise, you could leave the audience wondering about that question throughout, instead of listening to everything you are saying.

9. How do you think your audience will react? Will there be any hostility in the audience, do you think? If so, how can you prepare for that? Will they support what you have to say?

10. How would you like your audience to react? Visualise it.

Interview with
the Original 'Dragons'

In order to be the best pitch coach possible for the contestants on 'Dragons' Den', I needed to find out what the audience, the 'Dragons' in this case, wanted to hear. I interviewed the five original 'Dragons' in series one of the Irish 'Dragons' Den' – Bobby Kerr, Niall O'Farrell, Sarah Newman, Gavin Duffy and Seán Gallagher – to see what they were looking for in a pitch.

According to them, the two-minute pitch is essential if you are a potential entrepreneur. It is their first impression of you, and you have a slim chance of getting investment with a bad pitch. The pitch either turns the light on for them, or switches it off. It needs to contain the beginning, middle and end of the story. The two-minute pitch needs to be well presented and clearly spoken. A vital quality in the entrepreneur is to be clear and understandable. The worst thing you can do in a pitch is to lie or be disingenuous.

When a candidate enters the 'Den' and their pitch is flat, the 'Dragons', in turn, are also flat. The pitch really needs to grab their attention. Do not be worried about being nervous – the 'Dragons' still give a fair hearing to someone who is nervous. You need to explain your idea, product or service with clarity. You need to demonstrate its potential, make it attractive to an investor and show a return on investment. One of the things that really annoys them is when someone gives an outrageous valuation on their company.

Contestants need to clearly demonstrate in their pitch how

their idea differs from anything else on the market. What is the target market of the product, and how are they going to get it to that market? What is the investment required, and how are they going to generate profit as a viable business?

Do it your own way. The 'Dragons' are investing in you, not what you think their perception of you should be. Your natural charm should shine through as you let the investor know that you are passionate about your business.

You need to clearly state why you are there, what you have, what you want and why you want it. Then answer questions with honesty and clarity. Nerves are common. If you do not have nerves you can risk coming across as dull or boring. Take a deep breath. This should help you to relax. Be the best you can be and practise.

Four 'Dragons' Den' Contestants Share Their Experience

To give you a sense of what it feels like to pitch on 'Dragons' Den', I have interviewed four previous contestants on the programme.

Interview with John Joyce, 'Dragons' Den' Contestant 2011

John Joyce is CTO at Yvolution, which produces wheeled toys. John is also founder of Savvybear.com which designs educational computer games for children on the web and as an app. It is Savvybear.com that John pitched on 'Dragons' Den' in 2011. He was successful in gaining €80,000 investment on the day.

How did you prepare for your pitch?

Although I spent weeks and weeks preparing my pitch before the day itself, I was very nervous while waiting to go into the 'Den'. I found it very helpful to practise my pitch beforehand. It got my head into gear. It is like sports coaching, prepping you before you enter the field of play.

How did you remember your pitch?

I memorised my pitch and was very happy with the way I delivered it in the 'Den'. I was very nervous before I spoke, but once I got the first words out, all my nerves went.

Is there anything you would have done differently?

I would have spent more time training in front of a video camera.

What did you learn from the experience?

I learned that I can pitch really well. I just thought that I was an IT geek with an idea.

Are you glad you pitched on 'Dragons' Den'?

Yes and no. Yes, in that I needed money and support at that time. No, in that now I have more experience in raising capital, and I could have gone elsewhere.

Have you pitched since 'Dragons' Den'?

Since pitching on the television programme, I've done many pitches to VCs in the UK and USA. They are more difficult, as the stakes are higher. I raised €80,000 in the 'Den', but I raised millions in VC houses.

What advice would you give to anyone pitching on 'Dragons' Den'?

Get professional help. Practise like mad. Be brave. Be passionate. Know your stuff. I believe we all learn new things every year. I believe pitching is a difficult task for anyone. I think it is like any sport and you have to train to become good at it. I have also learned to act, and I mean act, as you will meet some difficult people during the pitching process, but keep your eye on the end line and act, spin, twist. Do whatever you have got to do to get the goal.

Interview with Siobhan King-Hughes, 'Dragons' Den' Contestant 2012

Siobhan is founder of Swift factory, specialising in mobile phone apps and cloud computing. She is also ex-CEO of Sensormind, the company she pitched on 'Dragons' Den' in 2012. Although Siobhan spent about a month preparing for the pitch, she did not get the investment of €100,000 that she was looking for.

How helpful was it to practise your pitch?

It is not just helpful to practise beforehand, it is essential. You only get one shot – there are no retakes in the 'Den'.

I knew we had to do a two-minute pitch with no notes or props – no PowerPoint, no cue cards. Although I knew my business really well and was reasonably comfortable with public speaking, I wanted to make sure that I got the main points across and was able to deliver the message with fluidity. I wrote the whole pitch out, and read it aloud with a timer to ensure it was timed right.

I ran through it with some trusted friends in advance, to practise projecting my voice and getting through without stopping.

How did you remember your pitch?

I used a recall method called the 'journey method' which I learned about from a book, *You Can Have an Amazing Memory*, by memory expert Dominic O'Brien. He described the method of creating a mental journey, and dropping items that you want to remember along the path. I dropped keywords from my speech onto a familiar 'mental path'. It meant that if I forgot one item I could move on with the next item in my pitch, rather than coming up blank and grinding to a halt, which, from experience, is what can happen if you have no plan.

Were you nervous?

I have never, ever been so nervous. My product set was arranged on a side table, covered by a cloth. The plan was to whip the cloth away and face the 'Dragons'. Unfortunately, when I pulled the cloth – the whole lot collapsed all over the floor! I just ignored it and kept going as if nothing had happened. What else can you do? At the end of the day, nothing ever goes 100 percent according to plan. You just have to roll with it sometimes.

What did you learn from the experience?

Although my slot on the show was less than ten minutes, in reality I spent almost two hours on my feet fielding questions from the 'Dragons' and surrounded by cameras. I learned what I am capable of, and I found out that I work quite well under pressure.

Were you happy with your pitch on the day?

I was happy with the way I delivered my pitch in the 'Den'. I got through the two minutes, and got rare praise from the 'Dragons' for delivering a solid pitch. I am really happy with the pitch itself – I do not think I would change a thing. My pitch coach was great – calm, which is what is needed. I would definitely recommend a memory technique so that if the worst happens and you go blank, you have a framework to carry you through.

I am delighted I pitched on the 'Den', it was a really fantastic experience. I would recommend it to anyone.

Have you pitched since 'Dragons' Den'?

I have had to pitch many times since the 'Den'. They have been much easier. No pitch has ever fazed me since the 'Den'.

What advice would you give to someone pitching in the 'Den'?

Know your stuff. While most investment pitches are time limited, the 'Dragons' can ask you anything and can keep you there for as long as it takes. You need to know your business well. If there is an aspect of the business that is not your core strength, bring a colleague who can speak to that section.

Prepare. You have nothing to lose and everything to gain by practicing in advance. You may be good at thinking on your feet, but practise anyway – you will come across as more polished.

Time yourself. Timing is really important. The pressure of the moment means you may talk faster than normal – or ramble.

Read or speak your pitch out loud, while standing up. There is a huge difference between quietly reading your notes to yourself in a chair, and standing up and projecting to a room full of people.

Delivering a pitch is not easy. Few of us are 'naturals', but you owe it to your audience to at least deliver professionally, and you owe it to yourself to present your business in the best possible light.

Interview with Tara Dalrymple, 'Dragons' Den' Contestant 2014

Tara Dalrymple is the founder of Feelsright. She pitched her business, Mission Possible, on 'Dragons' Den' in 2014. Feelsright is the same business as Mission Possible with a different name and branding. Tara was looking for a €50,000 investment from the 'Dragons' for five percent equity. Although she did not get investment on the day, Tara's business has soared since. She was named one of the 'Top 20 Tech Start-ups to Watch in 2015' by *Silicon Republic*.

What is Feelsright?

It is a cloud-based employee reward, compensation and recognition platform which enables companies to buy credit for their staff to delegate their personal to-do list to a community of locally verified service providers. This, in turn, increases staff productivity, gives workers a free and efficient way to maximise their work-life balance, and gives the service providers access to new clients as well as collecting their payments.

How did you prepare for your pitch?

I spent between two and three weeks preparing for my pitch before entering the 'Den', so I actually felt very confident while I was waiting to face the 'Dragons'. It was very important to practise my pitch beforehand, as I made many pivots during the morning, which added more punch to the pitch.

How did you remember your pitch?

I remembered my pitch by saying it out loud over and over again. I had had a practice run with five panel members for two hours the Friday before. I mainly learnt it off by heart, and then made changes accordingly. As a whole, I was happy with the way that I delivered my pitch in the 'Den'. There are definitely things I would change, but at the end of the day it is all relative to that moment in time.

Were you nervous?

I was the most nervous I have ever been. I love presenting and can talk away like anything, but 'Dragons Den' is like what kryptonite is to Superman: it drains you of all your powers and you really do not remember anything.

Were you happy with your pitch on the day?

Looking back, I would have changed my answers to some of their questions. I am glad I pitched on 'Dragons' Den', though. As an entrepreneur you have to put yourself out there, and it was all about the publicity and exposure.

Have you pitched since 'Dragons' Den'?

I have had to deliver a lot of pitches since 'Dragons' Den' – to Enterprise Ireland, to college students, at events – and I enjoyed them all. I love being given the opportunity to speak about the things I am passionate about: business and technology.

What advice would you give to anyone pitching on the 'Den'?

My advice would be the following: do a dry run with a panel

beforehand, made up of mentors, local business people or your advisory board, but definitely not friends and family – they will always tell you that it is great.

Interview with Ollie Fegan, 'Dragons' Den' Contestant 2013

Ollie's current business is a cinema app called Usheru. It is a different business to Tempster, which Ollie pitched on 'Dragons' Den' in 2013, but he says that 'the genesis for the idea came from Tempster'. Ollie received a €100,000 investment for twenty percent equity on 'Dragons' Den', though the investment did not ultimately go through.

How long did you spend preparing for your pitch?

I did not spend long enough preparing – I was certainly undercooked. A busy work schedule meant that I only really began to prepare two days before the pitch. I completely changed my pitch immediately beforehand, and focused on telling a story. I used keywords to help me remember the points I had to make, and, after a shaky start, the nerves left me and I got into a better flow.

Were you nervous beforehand?

It is hard to not be nervous waiting downstairs before you walk into the 'Den', but I believed in my product and was genuinely excited, so I had to channel that into positive nervous energy.

I was very nervous at the start in the 'Den' itself, but as the pitch went on, I was fine. I forgot that the cameras were there and treated it as I would a job interview.

Were you happy with your pitch in the 'Den'?

I would rate how happy I was with the performance as fifty-fifty. I think I started weakly, but when I got into showing the product it flowed a lot better.

What would you have done differently?

I have since given many pitches to far more unforgiving investors and panels. I have learned to put a lot more personality into the pitch, more tone, and focus on storytelling. People want to be entertained, and your personality and story need to really explain, in layman's terms, what your company does. Forget the jargon; connect and tell the story of the industry problem your business is going to solve. Practise a lot, too. People see an under-cooked pitch as a sign that you are not professional, or that you are not serious about what you are doing.

What did you learn from the experience?

It was early in my start-up journey, so I needed to learn a lot. The pitch, and, more specifically, your training, taught me to focus on connecting with the panel. Learn about them and their interests and know what you want to get from a pitch before you go in.

Are you happy you pitched on 'Dragons' Den'?

Yes, one hundred percent. It is not something I ever thought of doing and I applied on a whim. It was fun, and I loved the pressure-cooker environment.

Have you pitched since 'Dragons' Den'?

Yes, I have pitched many times since 'Dragons' Den'. I have honed my style a great deal. I have learned to focus on connecting with the audience and I have learned to find enjoyment in them.

What advice would you give to someone pitching on 'Dragons' Den'?

Have a good opening, and ask a question. Your audience have probably heard a fair few pitches before yours, so wake them up. A good question can also help make clear what industry you are in, and what the problem is that you are trying to solve. Focus first on the problem, and make it clear that there is a problem worth investing in. They want to invest in a painkiller – people tend to pay more for a painkiller than for a vitamin.

Then explain how you solve the problem. Explain how big the opportunity is, and why no one else can do it better. Acknowledge the competition, but explain why you and your team can crack it and how you will make money. Close your pitch by bringing it back to the problem, and why this solution is a game changer.

Chapter Four

IS NETWORKING JUST PITCHING, OR VICE VERSA?

I have never considered myself to be particularly good at networking. I do not have business cards, and I am not at business events seven nights a week. After speaking with Caitlin O'Connor, though, I realised that I was not too bad at it – it was as a result of networking that I gathered all the wonderful interviews for this book. A strong element of networking is asking. I simply asked the brilliant people I know.

Interview with Caitlin O'Connor, Innovation Strategist and Networking Expert

Are there different types of networking?

There are many different types of networking: one-to-one, one-to-many, referrals or strategic networking, and then casual networking, in which you might be attending a party, or social networking, which is online.

People often find casual or social networking quite difficult. They might ask, 'How do I tell friends who I'm sailing with or who I'm at a party with that I'm looking for business from them?' In fact, you don't. It is much slower, but there is more trust and it will probably lead to a much bigger engagement. You just keep sowing the seeds: what you are working on, what your challenges are, or how you have this amazing product. You are still pitching, but you are doing it in a more subliminal way. The 'in-your-face' pitching works well with venture capitalists – they want a quick win. They want to hear twenty or thirty pitches in one afternoon and then make a decision. It can be very different day-to-day, so you need to judge the tone and atmosphere.

When two or more people meet, you have an opportunity to network. Every time you have the opportunity to meet someone, you have the opportunity to plant that seed that is part of your pitch. You might drop something into conversation like, 'I was really busy today as I was doing a tender on building swimming pools.' Then the person you are in conversation with knows that you build swimming pools. It is all pitching, just at different levels of depth and tone.

Can you network to get a job?

Eighty percent of people get a job through someone they know. Somebody might have told them about the application, or somebody might have introduced them to someone else in-house, but most jobs are sourced through networking.

Going for an interview, you have got to know what the interviewer wants. You have the job description so you have a fair idea what they want. You might know some of the challenges they face in their business, and you may have networked your way around the organisation to find out what the motivating factors that drive these people are. It is very important that you network your way around to actually find out that information.

How important is it to ask?

Asking is one very big part of networking. Ask for what you want, but know that you have got to be capable of following through. You have to be ready to act on what you have asked for. In Ireland – in the country more so than in the cities – farmers do all their work through networking. They buy a bull or sell a bull, or whatever it might be, entirely through networking. I think we unlearnt this in the cities, and forgot how to ask for what we are looking for. Networking is not about selling – it is about communicating what you do, where you are going, what you want and how somebody can help you. We cannot expect people to be mind readers or fortune tellers, assuming that they know what we want when we have not actually asked them. You might be surprised by what comes out when you ask someone directly.

Networking is really about asking and pitching in a more gentle way, as you are not there to sell and it is very off-putting if somebody breathes down your throat as if they were pitching to a hundred venture capitalists in one room. You need to have thought about who your target market is, what you are communicating, what is in it for the other person and how you can engage with that person. But remember that it is still pitching.

Can you give an example of what you do in networking training?

Networking is a core area of who I am, both up to now and going forward. In my networking training courses, I use a game with a ball of wool and ten people or so in a circle. Someone has to start with the ball of wool and say, for example, 'My name is Caitlin O'Connor, my area of expertise is networking and I am looking to connect with a corporate company that needs networking training.' We never stall in this game, as everyone knows somebody who can help them.

There was one course that I did with a group of lawyers, during which one of the women said, 'I want to be connected with the managing director of a pharmaceutical company, ideally in Ireland, but anywhere in the world.' There was a deafening silence. Twenty seconds felt like a year. And then, the next thing I knew was that another girl said, 'I can introduce you to my dad. He's the managing director of a pharmaceutical company in Mayo.' And the first girl got up, put her hands on her hips and said, 'Why did you never tell me that before?' And, of course, the answer was, 'You never asked.'

How important is listening in networking?

Listening is really important in networking. When you rearrange the word 'listen' you get the word 'silent'. We do not listen if we are not silent. It is a specifically Irish trait to 'butt in'. You really need to glue your tongue to the roof of your mouth to stop yourself talking. I think you have got to listen to the person you are meeting with. Sometimes you realise from listening that no opportunity exists for you at that moment, but you are still building a network for the future. Indeed, you may be able to make a referral then and there, or at some point in the future that contributes to your networking strategy.

How can you influence people?

I think you can influence people through storytelling. For example, 'Do you see Joe over there? Well, we did X for Joe, and this is what happened. He saved fifty-two percent on whatever.' Storytelling and testimonials are a great way of influencing people, but so is putting yourself in their shoes, showing empathy and thinking, 'What would they get out of this? How easy would it be to engage?' Romantic coaches ask, 'Would you date yourself?' You need to ask, 'Would I give business to myself?'

We influence, as well, by quick communication. One of the ways that I got a lot of business over the years was that I worked long hours, but also responded to proposals I received within that same day. Responding to communication quickly builds trust. You tend not to buy from somebody that you do not trust.

How important is the emotional connection?

The emotional connection is really important when networking or pitching. A lot of people buy with their emotions. We either buy with our head or our heart, it is fifty-fifty. You do not know what fifty percent you are talking to – whether they are buying with their head or their heart – and some people just buy from people they like. If you have made a good pitch, smiled and exchanged pleasantries, and if they like you and they feel like they can trust you, then if they want to give business to you they will.

How can you build your network?

It is really important that you keep building your network as you go. My network is very large, because I have been networking for twenty years. I am now working on a project where I need to engage with between thirty and fifty international corporates, and I had no problem with that, because a lot of these people are CEOs of companies who I had previously engaged with. I never knew when I was actually going to need to contact them again, but that initial relationship is of value. So even though what you are pitching may not be of relevance to somebody right now, it is important to communicate with them and to engage with them, because you do not know when they (or you) will be in a different role, or how your paths will cross. Many years ago a boss of mine said: 'The penny is very round.'

I was recently pitching a project to thirty companies, and I went to the CEO, the managing director or director in each one of those companies. They are the decision makers. Of course, sometimes there are others who make decisions. I have worked with many different companies in which it might actually be the sales director or the marketing director who has made the decision, rather than the investor or the CEO or managing director. You have got to know who the decision maker is, and who holds the purse strings.

Do you have a formula for a pitch?

No, I do not necessarily have a formula for a pitch. Sometimes I go into companies and it is more like a conversation, sitting down and having a coffee. I therefore have to sense the mood. I would sense, as the conversation went on, what their challenges were, how I could engage with them, and whether it was appropriate to go harder or softer. It is often a case of treading softly, because you want to build the relationship first. I might build the relationship in the first or the second meeting, so it would only be at a later stage that I ask for something.

Would you use slides in a meeting?

If I had a meeting I would never go in with PowerPoint slides. They can be very formal, when the first meeting should be about engagement and developing the relationship. It is important to keep in touch with those that you have done work with because you never know where they are going to end up. I am currently doing some work in the UK with a guy who I have done some work with here in Ireland. We had a conversation, and from that there came a statement of requirement from him talking about what they needed. We then reached the proposal and pitch stage, but at the beginning it was all very casual.

When are you pitching?

You have got to be aware that you are always pitching. You always have to be prepared, but you go in with different tones at the ready, be it casual or strategic. You can never let your hair down. Every single engagement is a pitch of some sort or another, because you are looking for something. If you are an entrepreneur, you never take that hat off. If you are in business and employed you can take that hat off at the weekends, but if you are self-employed, you never take that hat off.

Chapter Five

INVESTMENT PITCHING – GOVERNMENT SUPPORTS

Is there any difference between pitching to the 'Dragons' and any other investment pitch? Without television cameras and five 'Dragons', I believe it can only get easier. Investment pitches can take many shapes and forms. If you are just starting off in business, you may end up pitching to your Local Enterprise Office or Enterprise Ireland for financial support or investment. You could also pitch to get on to New Frontiers, Enterprise Ireland's national entrepreneur-development programme for innovative, early-stage start-ups.

I have previously worked as a mentor with Fingal Local Enterprise Office in north Dublin, where clients were assigned to me for coaching on an important pitch they had for their business. I have also sat in on advice clinics, where people made a thirty-minute appointment to pitch their idea for a business, often for the very first time. I remember one lady coming to me during an advice clinic a couple of years ago, who had what I thought was a great idea for summer camps with a difference for kids. However, she lacked confidence. I suggested that she stand up against the wall in the little room we were in, with her shoulders back against the wall to improve her posture. She tried it and it worked. We practised the delivery of her message through variation in her voice, as well as having better eye contact. There was only so much I could do in thirty minutes, though, and I recommended her for further assistance with the Local Enterprise Office. I did not see her again until I was at a business event a few weeks ago, when I heard her name being called out for a prize in a raffle. I recognised her name, but I would never have recognised her. I introduced myself – she was so thrilled to see me, and oozing confidence. Her business was thriving, and she thanked me for believing in her during that initial meeting.

Local Enterprise Office

The Local Enterprise Office (LEO) is the 'first-stop shop' for anyone seeking information and support on starting or growing a business in Ireland. There are thirty-one Local Enterprise Offices around Ireland, providing advice, information and support in starting or growing your business.

Interview with Eibhlin Curley, Head of Enterprise, Local Enterprise Office Dún Laoghaire Rathdown

Do you assess many pitches?

I am regularly on the assessment panel for New Frontiers (the Hothouse Programme). I have also been on the Enterprise Ireland grants panel for Competitive Feasibility Funding, and on the Bank of Ireland Start-Up Awards Panel. I have been a judge for the LEO Student Enterprise Awards and for the Ireland's Best Young Entrepreneur competition, and have assessed over 100 business pitches in my career to date.

What are you looking for in the content of a pitch?

There are a few important questions that I look to be answered in a pitch.

- What is the customer need that they are addressing? What is the size of the market opportunity, and what paying customers (ideally) do they have?

- What is their business model? How will they make money? What is the sales cycle? What are the payment terms?

- What is their route to market, their marketing strategy and budget?

- What is their unique value proposition? Who are their competitors, and where are they located?

- Who is on the team? What is their commitment? What shareholding and roles do they have? How many employees will they have in the next three years?

- What is their export potential? How will they scale the business? How will they fund the business?

- How much money do they need, and for what exactly? Who else is funding the business? What are their financial projections for the next three years?

What are you mainly looking for in the selection process for funding?

I look for credibility in the entrepreneur and team, and commercial viability within a sustainable and scalable business model.

What tips would you give for a good pitch?

- Explain your track record, industry experience, qualifications, previous awards and identify other funders and paying or reference customers. Give realistic market analysis and financial forecasts.

- Clearly communicate how the business will make money and is better than competitors. Illustrate with examples.

- Explain what your business does in non-technical terms and describe the customer benefits not the product features.

- Clear, relevant images, graphics or short videos can be useful, if using slides.

- Avoid small and crowded text on presentations.

- A prototype or drawing of the product can be useful if appropriate.

Do you invest in the idea or in the person?

They are both important. The market opportunity is important too.

Is the delivery of the pitch important?

- The delivery style is very important in communicating your message, engaging your audience and building a rapport and credibility.

- Speak slowly, clearly and loudly enough for your audience to hear and understand you easily. Try to engage your audience with eye contact and positive body language and posture.

- Bring a bottle of water with you in case your mouth goes dry, or even to steady your nerves.

- Energy and enthusiasm help in the delivery of the pitch. Pitching-assessment days tend to be long and intensive for the judges, who will sometimes listen to around twelve pitches in one sitting.

What presentation format do you prefer?

Presentation formats should facilitate the delivery of your message, and not distract the audience. Try to ensure that your presentation format will work on the available equipment, or bring your own device with suitable adaptors, especially if you are using an Apple Mac.

Is it essential to use slides?

Visuals are useful, even if there is no text. People absorb information in different ways: 'Visual' (with props and images), 'Aural', 'Read/Write' or 'Kinaesthetic' (using demonstrations). If appropriate, try to use some or all of these means of communicating.

How important is the start-up story?

It depends on the time frame and context – sometimes it is useful to explain the background and inspiration, but it should be kept short and relevant.

What advice would you give to potential pitchers?

Be clear about the purpose of your pitch, and make it relevant to your audience. If you are pitching for investment the focus is on what funding you need, what you will spend it on, how your business will make money and what the return is for the investor. Make sure you include realistic, accurate and relevant financial information that you can explain. It does not inspire confidence if your figures do not make sense.

Practise again and again – practise in front of a mirror, or take a video of yourself. Take feedback on board. Learn and move on. Under promise and over-deliver.

New Frontiers

Enterprise Ireland's New Frontiers programmes provide a full range of supports for the entrepreneur to develop themselves and their business proposition, progressing to being market-and investment-ready within six to nine months. I work as a pitch coach on nine of these programmes across Ireland, and the standard of start-ups I meet is increasing all the time.

Interview with Colm Ó Maolmhuire, Programme Manager, New Frontiers (NF), IT Tallaght

Can you tell us about New Frontiers in IT Tallaght?

New Frontiers is a collaborative programme between IT Tallaght and IT Blanchardstown. We run two cycles per annum: Phase 1 and Phase 2. In 2014, we received over sixty enquiries for the twenty-two places on the Phase 1 programme. There were over forty formal applications for the twelve places on Phase 2.

What are you looking for when assessing prospective participants for this programme?

Once a business idea or proposition is eligible, we look for inno-vation, growth potential, ambition, good business acumen and an ability to communicate clearly with customers, team and investors – or at least evidence of the potential ability to do so.

How important is it to be able to pitch?

Being able to pitch is an important part of the programme. We are preparing entrepreneurs to scale their businesses. They will not do that without a clear offering and the ability to convince others. Pitching is a vital element for any successful New Frontiers participant.

What are you looking for in a pitch?

A good pitch needs to excite the investor's interest, engage them and make them ask for more information. Confidence and trust in the promoter's abilities is key. A good pitch needs to sell the business, not just the product. It should start with an exciting outcome. There should be a clear definition of what it is that they are promoting, followed by clear market knowledge, good revenue and profit analysis as well as the team to deliver.

Do you invest in the person, the idea or both?

A very good person and/or team with a good idea is more important than a wonderful idea that cannot be executed.

How important is the delivery style?

The delivery style in a pitch is very important. You need to have confidence in yourself and your offering, and demonstrate credibility by showing your knowledge and getting the investor excited by your passion.

The person and proposition are more important than the

medium they use to present it. I have no preference for PowerPoint, Prezi or Keynote, but a tech-based entrepreneur should be competent with technology. I never recommend pitching without slides, as the audience need something else to look at besides you.

How important is the start-up story?

The start-up story is very important – investors buy into people as much as they buy into the technology or product.

What are the common mistakes that start-ups make?

The main mistakes that start-ups make in a pitch are being unprepared, lacking a clear message or purpose to each pitch, having too much text or too many visuals, being too long or having no specific 'ask'.

What tips could you give?

Practise and record the pitch, research the audience, have a purpose and plan for each pitch and be yourself – but your professional self.

Enterprise Ireland

Enterprise Ireland (EI) is the government organisation responsible for the development and growth of Irish enterprises in world markets. Many of the start-ups I meet on the New Frontiers programmes apply for funding from Enterprise Ireland. The main types of funding offered by Enterprise Ireland to start-up companies are ordinary shares for Competitive Start Fund (CSF) companies, where funding is limited to €50,000 for ten percent equity, or Convertible Preference shares for High Potential Start-Up (HPSU) companies, where funding is normally in excess of €200,000.

Interview with
Siobhan King-Hughes

Siobhan King-Hughes provides unique insight, as she has sat on both sides of the table. She was a contestant on 'Dragons' Den' in 2012, and she has been on the assessment panel of Enterprise Ireland's Competitive Start Fund (CSF) since July 2013.

At what stage should a start-up apply for funding from this fund?

The fund is for early stage start-ups, so you are not expected to have already proven your solution in the market, but you ought to be able to demonstrate that there is an appetite for the solution you are offering, and that you are capable of delivering it.

What is the calibre of the pitches you see for this fund?

The calibre of pitches is increasing all the time. Although the application process is relatively simple and decisions are made quickly, the competition is strong.

What content do you expect in a pitch, and in what order?

There is a selection process prior to the pitch day itself. As part of the application process, applicants are expected to deliver a video pitch. You will be asked to complete a six-to-eight-minute online video interview/pitch which will be viewed by the evaluation panel as part of the evaluation process. This video pitch is mandatory. Twenty-five percent of the overall marks are allocated to this submission. You will be asked to address the following questions:

- What are you going to sell?
- Who are you going to sell it to?
- Why are they going to buy it from you?
- How are you going to sell it to them?
- How are you going to make money?

You will also be given, at most, two minutes to add any additional comments. The video pitch is delivered through an automated system. Applicants should practise in advance so as to give the best possible presentation.

What advice can you give when pitching?

Once selected for the pitch day, applicants need to be pretty organised. While I have been on the panel, the pitch itself is only three-minutes long, with about ten minutes for questions. Entrepreneurs need to be able to deliver their idea, market and team succinctly in this tight time frame.

Because the pitch is so short, it is necessary to convey:

- What specific need your product addresses, and why someone would be 'compelled' to buy from you?
- What is it about you/your team that makes you capable?
- What would be the impact of €50,000 on your plan?

Do you invest in the idea or the person, or both?

Applicants are scored against the questions above (the idea, the team and the impact of a €50,000 investment). All of these combine to make a good investment proposition.

How important is delivery style in a pitch?

It is important to come across as competent and capable. Stand up, look the investor in the eye and present your idea. If you sit down and read your pitch you will not come across as investable. Approximately eighty percent of applicants do not make it to pitch day; if you are in the twenty percent that makes it – put your best foot forward.

What presentation format do you prefer?

The method of delivery is not important. What is important is the content.

Do start-ups ever pitch to you without slides?

Yes. This can work if the promoter stands up, moves about and is particularly engaging, otherwise it may come off as 'unprepared'. It can also work if there is a physical product to look at or examine. In general though, slides seem to help keep promoters on message, as long as they are not flooded with eight-point type which the promoter decides to read.

How important is the start-up story?

As time is limited, there is not much opportunity to delve into backstory. If the promoters have history (previous start-up experience, good or bad, is always useful), mention it. If there is a powerful reason for starting this business, say so, and then move on. Every word must be relevant, or else should be left out.

What are the main mistakes that start-ups make in a pitch?

- Time management: I have seen many a pitch run out of time on slides. We see thirty companies in one day. If your pitch runs on, we will cut you off.

- Rambling off message: stick to the point you are trying to get across.

- Focusing on the technical rather than the market: your idea is cool, but would someone pay for it? How will you reach them?

What pitching advice would you give to start-ups?

- Stick to the timing.

- Know your message and get that message across.

- Practise in advance.

Interview with John O'Sullivan, Senior Portfolio Manager with Enterprise Ireland (EI)

John O'Sullivan manages a portfolio of 400-plus direct equity investments in SMEs and large companies.

What is the range of funding that EI offers a start-up?

The range of equity funding offered by Enterprise Ireland starts at €50,000 for Competitive Start Fund (CSF) companies, and goes up to €1.2 million for High-Potential Start-Up (HPSU) companies, depending on their innovation status and the region in which they are located. For companies older than five years, funding can be provided against qualified expenditure; the amount of funding obtainable will be further determined by the location of the company and associated commercial risks.

What are the main criteria for a high potential start-up to apply for EI funding?

For high potential start-up (HPSU) companies, they must be seeking to generate €1 million plus in revenues within three years, with the majority being from exports. They must also be seeking to employ ten or more staff within the three years.

Does the start-up have to match the funding?

Enterprise Ireland seeks that companies can raise matching funding from new or existing shareholders, with the exception of CSF companies, who are required to provide €5,000 in matching funds.

How many people would normally sit on the panel for funding?

There are nine Enterprise Ireland investment committee members, plus the committee secretary.

Who would typically make up the panel?

The Enterprise Ireland investment committee is made up of members of Enterprise Ireland's internal senior management team and external committee members.

At what stage should a start-up be, in order to apply for funding from Enterprise Ireland?

The funding supports available from Enterprise Ireland depend on the stage of development of the company, and the amount of matching funds that the start-up can raise. For very early-stage start-ups that have limited capacity to raise matching funds, CSF funding might be appropriate. For start-ups that can raise larger amounts of matching funding, HPSU funding would be an option, provided the company can demonstrate that it is capable of raising the required funding to deliver on its business plan, seek to generate the majority of its revenues from exports, will be undertaking R&D, has the potential to achieve €1 million-plus in revenues within three years and will employ ten or more staff within three years.

What is the calibre of the pitches you see?

They are usually of varied quality, with the weaker pitches focusing solely on the technical aspects of the product or service. The stronger pitches have a greater focus on the market opportunity, the problems that the product and/or service will solve for customers and how the funding will help deliver value for shareholders.

What content do you expect in a pitch, and in what order?

The content of the pitch should be largely decided by the audience being pitched to, and the length of time available to pitch. The strongest pitches are usually the ones that incorporate the following points:

1. The promoter's experience and/or track record.

2. What market gap has been identified for their product and/or service.

3. How the funding being pitched for will help deliver on the business plan, preferably with some milestones targets to be achieved.

4. Post funding, where the promoter envisages the company being in three to five years, and how this will generate shareholder value.

Do you invest in the idea or the person, or both?

If a promoter has a strong commercial background it generally provides increased comfort for investors, especially if they have been successful in previous ventures. If the idea is also compelling then both elements will likely result in an investment, as it lowers the risk profile for an investor. If the promoter has limited commercial experience but a compelling idea, then they can strengthen their investor proposal by seeking to appoint an experienced advisory committee and/or advisors with financial and/or start-up experience.

How important is delivery style in a pitch?

It is very important. If a pitch is delivered badly it reduces an investor's trust in the promoter, and when in a competitive pitch environment with other start-ups it can reduce the chances of winning an investment approval.

It is always beneficial to practise for a pitch in advance with an advisor or friend that will provide constructive criticism where required. When listening to a pitch, you are both listening to the content and observing the delivery style. An investor is looking for pitch variances that might indicate potential credibility issues with the business proposition. If a promoter can convey a confident pitch they will have a greater chance of being successful and/or being offered a follow-up meeting.

What presentation format do you prefer?

The more graphic, less wordy style of presentation is generally the preferred style for most investors. For graphic presentations, Prezi is probably the most visually strong in terms of demonstrating your pitch.

Do start-ups ever pitch to you without slides?

Promoters will seek to pitch without slides on occasion, but it is always preferable to pitch with slides, as it makes for a more compelling pitch. If it is an informal pitch at a conference or networking event then it is preferable to pitch without slides, as an investor does generally not want to carry around slides at an event. The pitch should be aimed at trying to arrange a formal meeting, where a formal presentation can be pitched to the investor.

How important is the start-up story?

The start-up story is important, as it shows the evolution of the company from concept to incorporation. If the story is compelling it increases the credibility of the company and its business proposition. If the start-up story is not overly compelling then the focus should shift to the compelling business opportunity that the start-up is trying to capture.

What are the main mistakes that start-ups make in a pitch?

The main mistakes are not being prepared for the pitch, not engaging with the audience, focusing too much on the technical aspects of the business, not focusing on how the company will gain commercial traction or who the target customer is and, finally, being overly ambitious with future sales. If a promoter can show that they understand the challenges of generating large sales for an unproven start-up, and that it will take time and resources to scale, then they will generally increase their credibility with the investor and lower the risk profile of the company.

What tips or advice would you give to start-ups regarding their pitch?

I would recommend practising your pitch in advance with someone who will give you credible feedback, then re-pitching until you are satisfied with the delivery. I would also recommend tailoring your pitch to your prospective audience by researching the audience in advance. If the audience is technically proficient, then present a technically orientated pitch. If it is an investor audience, then pitch to demonstrate the commercial opportunity. I would also recommend keeping track of the time when pitching, especially in a competitive pitching environment with limited time available to pitch.

Chapter Six

INVESTMENT PITCHING: ACCELERATOR PROGRAMMES

Accelerator programmes are springing up all over Ireland and internationally. These are privately funded programmes that help a start-up or early stage business. The focus of an accelerator programme is on rapid growth, and it helps to sort out any organisational, operational and strategic challenges facing the business. Firstly, you will have to pitch to a panel of industry experts in order to get onto one of these programmes. At the end of an accelerator programme, you are often expected to pitch to an audience of hundreds as part of a pitch competition or demo day. This audience could be made up of a combination of journalists, venture capitalists, judges and media.

My first experience of one of these events was in Dublin in February 2013. I was in Today FM for a radio interview, based on an article I had written for the *Irish Independent*'s 'Health and Living' section, on the wait times for nursing homes. My friend from college, Juliette Gash, is a broadcast journalist with Today FM and we met for a coffee and catch-up afterwards. Juliette told me about a press release that had just come in for a networking event called 'Pitchify', to be held in the Odeon on Harcourt Street in Dublin the following evening. There would be six three-minute elevator pitches from start-ups, followed by a keynote speaker.

I contacted Brian Daly, co-founder of Pitchify, and offered my service as a pitch coach for the event. I listened to the six pitches an hour before the event and gave some coaching on their delivery. The keynote speaker for the event was Catherine Flynn, global marketing manager for Facebook. Brian asked me if I would be a guest speaker and share some tips on pitching. Trustev from Cork was one of the start-ups pitching that evening, and they were in the early stages of their success. By the time we came downstairs from the practice session in the Odeon the place was hopping. Over 750 entrepreneurs, venture capitalists and media turned up on the night. With due credit to Brian and his team, it was a free event, and all of the advertising was done through social media.

Following on from his success with Pitchify, Brian went on to work with the Web Summit in Dublin, and then Techstars in London. He is currently working with Techstars Berlin, 'Europe's hottest accelerator', as he calls it.

'Pitching is all about presenting the "wow" factor,' says Brian. 'People – especially investors – do not care about what you are doing. They care about what you have done.'

★

Simon Cocking is the founder, mentor and senior editor of Irish Tech News. Simon has pitched to all kinds of decision makers in business, as well as to public stakeholders (ministers, TDs, local politicians, residents, planners) and to UCD's Innovation Academy and the Digital Skills Academy. Simon is also a judge for pitch competitions on start-up and accelerator programmes, most recently for 'Sprinters', a three-day start-up sprint for women, and the Web Summit 'PITCH' 2015 event.

Simon's pitching tips come from his blog in the New Frontiers online publication, 2 June 2015, titled 'Pitching: avoiding the pitfalls and answering the right questions'.

What problem are you solving?

Tell us early and clearly.

Who are you, and what is your company name?

I saw someone the other day who seemed interesting, had already sold a previous company for seven figures and yet still did not clearly say the name of his company, and mumbled his own.

What do you want?

Clearly tell us what you are looking for, and what sort of help you need – financial, technical or other.

History. Briefly, please!

Your backstory can be interesting, but should never dominate the pitch or take up too much time. Tell us enough, but not so much that we are wondering what you are here for today.

Do not be surprised by the content of your slides.

This might sound obvious, but people get tripped up again and again by the wrong slides loading, or seeing images they did not expect.

Do not have ugly, text-heavy slides.

Slides should just be a visual prompt. You can read, we can read, we do not need you to read off the content of your slides. One word, or only a few, is plenty. Less is so much more.

Do not read your presentation from hand-held notes. It looks bad, and it means that you are not looking at your audience. You do not need to follow an exact script, you need to use the slides as a visual path to take you through a series of concepts. This means that you will need to learn your content, and that is part of pitching.

Rehearse, rehearse, rehearse. And know how long your pitch takes.

Yes, we all hate practising our pitch, but just accept that it is part of what you need to do. Also, it gets better the second and third times. You will work out where you are stumbling, and what you need to articulate more clearly. It is well worth the time you put into it.

No TLAs (three-letter acronyms)

One team once went to the US and said, 'Hi, we're an EI-backed HPSU.' Speak in plain English. You gain nothing by overcomplicating your delivery. It is far smarter to be able to explain your concept simply: 'We do x, which solves y.'

Find a devil's advocate.

Think about the weak points in your project, then think through good answers to these challenges. You do not need to have a complete answer to everything, but you should demonstrate that you are aware of these risks, and have considered possible strategies to deal with them.

Be happy and relaxed. This is not the worst thing you could be doing!

It is true that many people hate public speaking. If you are one of these people, then start finding opportunities to do exactly that – it is not going to go away. If you want to succeed in business, you will need to explain to others why they should give you their money and/or expertise.

Below is an interview with Wayne Murphy, an accelerator programme director. Wayne is director of the Bank of Ireland accelerator, Start Planet, and Start Planet Northern Ireland (NI). I had the pleasure of working with Wayne as a pitch coach on the Bank of Ireland accelerator.

Interview with Wayne Murphy, Accelerator Programme Director at Start Planet NI

There are many factors that dictate the success of a business, and much of it involves emotion. Ultimately, what is it that drives a potential customer to make that decision to buy a product? It is an emotional need or an attachment. The most successful companies in the world are excellent when it comes to figuring out that 'buying trigger'. A good story well told can have an amazing effect on a pitch audience so preparation is the price paid for superiority.

A pitch is all about attracting a potential customer to buy your organisation, your idea, your people, your product, your service and your potential. That 'customer' can be an investor, a partner, an actual or potential buyer of your product or indeed an advisor or network you need to be part of. Accordingly, you need to focus on the key strengths of your start-up, be that your intellectual property (IP), your tech ability, your network or your incredibly disruptive idea.

When pitching, most start-ups get too complicated and include far too much information. Pitching really is an art. It needs to have five key elements: to be simple, personal, emotional and credible, and have the ability to connect with the audience in some way. It is the story of your journey, a familiar one to you, of course, and it must also include what has driven you to take this journey and portray the personal 'mission', tenacity, drive and commitment to succeed. It needs to demonstrate passion, as it needs to bring people with you on your journey. It needs to describe what the big problem is, and how you and your team are solving it. It needs to be focused on your intended audience. A pitch is all about clearly identifying and/or creating the needs of a customer.

Successful pitches focus primarily on the customer, knowing the market and how you and your business can make their lives much easier, more productive or happier. Focusing on the customer should at all times be the central focus of a pitch, no matter what the 'ask'. There is no better validation of your meeting a need than a customer buying your product. Customer validation attracts investment, and any pitch 'ask' should be further investment to simply enable you to increase the number of customers you have.

Always focus on the customer. Be emotional about it and the investment will follow.

★

Joshua Henderson is vice president of Springboard Enterprises in Washington DC. He is a founding board member at Women in Healthcare and Life Sciences. Joshua's mission is to promote, inspire and increase the odds of success for women entrepreneurial leaders. Joshua has managed the global expert network for Women in Healthcare and Life Sciences, and has run accelerator programmes in the digital media, entertainment, consumer Internet, clean technology, healthcare and life-science sectors for over seven years. In his blog post, published on 20 May 2014, Joshua suggests five things you should not forget when pitching to investors. Joshua's blog is joshuahenderson.com.

Do not forget that the first pitch is the trailer, not a full-length film.

Solution: Focus on highlights and creating interest for a follow-up meeting. Pitch sessions like the ones we run at Springboard are opportunities to start or build relationships. Success is pitching an interesting enough story to warrant a follow-up meeting. Hook them with your trailer, and they will want to see the feature-length film.

Do not spend too much time on the product, and not enough on the business.

Solution: Get to the point faster. Too many entrepreneurs are in love with their product, and it often comes through in the investor pitch. Remember that you need to speak the language of the investor, not the customer. The core interests of your target audience are different, which means that the key messages of the pitch should be different.

Investors are interested in the business case, and in the return on their investment. They need to know how you make money, your assumptions around the go-to-market approach and speed-to-scale that are represented in your financials, and the key value-inflecting milestones that this round (and future rounds needed) will buy them en route to potential exit opportunities where the investor will realise their return.

Do not be uninteresting.

Solution: incorporate storytelling. While actual numbers vary by individual and firm, you can be sure that you are not the only investment opportunity an investor will see that week. You are one of many, and yet from your perspective you are the only one.

Remember the importance of first impressions, and the importance that investors place on likability. Telling a story makes you human. People like to invest in humans (they 'bet on the jockey not the horse'). If you focus only on the facts and the business, and do not give the sense of where you draw your passion from, investors will not walk away from your pitch thinking that you are unstoppable. Be unstoppable.

Do not forget to say what the company does.

Solution: This should be the first thing out of your mouth. Develop a one-to-two-line summary of what your company does, and say it in the first thirty seconds of any pitch that you give.

At Springboard we run many sessions that include a pitch followed by a Q&A and feedback. You would be shocked by how often the first comment after a pitch is to say, 'I still do not understand exactly what your company does.' When a pitch fails to clearly communicate what the company does, or waits until a minute or two into the pitch to tell me, I find myself hung up on that question, craving the answer and unable to focus on anything else in the presentation. Your summary statement is the bedrock on which everything else is built.

Do not forget to focus on one key takeaway.

Solution: Think of your calling card. We work with entrepreneurs on a ten-minute investor pitch. Among other things, we advocate for simple, visual slides with titles that spoon-feed the audience each slide's key takeaway. But even in a ten-slide deck, ten takeaways are too many. Cognitive psychology tells us that the number of points people can remember during a presentation is closer to three. You could think carefully about what your three key takeaways will be, and embed them as themes throughout the pitch.

I would recommend you pick just one. Is it the early exit opportunities? Is it the team that has worked together with similar technology in an adjacent industry? Is it the massive opportunity?

Pick one, and make sure that your audience will never forget it. Reinforce it throughout the pitch so that the takeaway is actually taken away, because if they do, they will tell their partners, and next thing you know you'll have the follow-up meeting you wanted.

Interview with Andy Shannon, Head of Startupbootcamp Global

I came across Startupbootcamp online, and sent an e-mail requesting an interview. Andy kindly obliged.

Can you tell me a little about Startupbootcamp?

Startupbootcamp was founded in 2010, with our first programme in Copenhagen. We have quickly grown to eleven accelerator programmes in eight countries and, in total, have invested in 288 start-ups across more than thirty countries, making us the largest early stage investor outside of the US. What makes Startupbootcamp unique is that each of our eleven programmes invests in a specific industry, for example, Fintech in Singapore, or e-commerce in Amsterdam. Out of the hundreds of applicants, we invest in about ten start-ups per programme that are introduced to the most applicable mentors, investors, and partners in their industry. This kind of targeted access often takes companies years to achieve.

What are you looking for in the selection process to get into Startupbootcamp?

Above all else we are looking for founders who are passionate about solving a unique and challenging problem. Although we look at start-ups of all stages, the earliest stage a start-up enters our programme is typically at a) having a core team with diverse skill sets in place, and b) having a product built that initial customers are using.

Is being able to pitch an important part of Startupbootcamp?

Start-ups enter our programmes at many different ability levels, especially in how they communicate what they are doing. We have learnt that most people (including investors) do not really want to be 'pitched', so most of our focus is on helping a founder tell their story in a concise and passionate way. Even during our 'selection days' where start-ups meet over fifty mentors, we encourage start-ups to introduce themselves to the group, as opposed to a traditional 'pitch'. During the three-month programme, each team works with various coaches who help them with everything from communicating with investors to inspiring their team.

What, in your opinion, makes a good pitch?

There is no doubt that any time a start-up speaks with a mentor, investor, or large group, they need to make a connection with the audience. This typically involves sharing their founding story and vision for the future. Being relatable and using humour normally helps form an audience connection, and credibility can be built through understanding a company's key metrics and demonstrating learnings/improvements around these metrics.

What should be included?

The top three categories that come to mind for when a founder talks about their company are:

1. What the problem is and why it is painful;

2. What solution the company is giving, and how it is solving this problem; and

3. Quantifiably demonstrating that the company is making strides towards growing their key metrics.

How successful are your participants in Startupbootcamp in gaining investment?

While we prefer to focus on more fundamental metrics such as the number of mentors or partnerships, we are proud that seventy-three percent of Startupbootcamp start-ups raise, on average, €600,000, and that more than eighty percent are still operating.

From your experience, do venture capitalists invest in the idea or the person, or both?

From my experience venture capitalists understand that any young business is in a search of a sustainable and repeatable business model. While the idea is important, the key is a team that is passionate, can learn quickly and adapt to constantly changing market conditions.

How important is delivery style in a pitch, in terms of posture, eye contact, gestures, variation of pitch and pace of voice?

It is important for start-up founders to be themselves. Things like posture, eye contact, and other presentation styles improve through practice, so at Startupbootcamp we focus on continuously exposing founders to opportunities for them to improve the way they communicate about their company.

Do you prefer PowerPoint, Keynote or Prezi?

It is not about the tool used, but about the way the information is presented, formatted and delivered. I have personally used all three of the tools you mentioned, but I actually prefer Google Presentation for its ability to collaborate when creating a presentation.

Do you ever recommend pitching without slides?

I think slides that focus on visuals can be a good way of communicating a story. Even the best presenters I have seen use slides, often without any text.

How important is the start-up story?

A start-up's story is very important, maybe even the most important for young companies. Every founder should be able to articulate when their big 'aha!' moment happened, the personal inspiration behind it and how they are different from their competition. Remember that stories are the cornerstone of any business, whether it is sales, recruiting or raising funding.

What are the main mistakes that start-ups make in a pitch?

Start-ups tend to struggle when they jump right to their technical solution without talking about the problem in a relatable manner. While the solution and proprietary technology is important, it is normally much more impactful when weaved into a more holistic story surrounding a team and their vision for solving a problem.

What tips or advice would you give to start-ups regarding their pitch?

Be yourself, tell your story, and do not assume that you will be great right away – like everything, practice makes perfect.

Chapter Seven

HOW DO YOU ACCESS VENTURE CAPITAL?

Many start-ups survive and grow without investment from venture capitalists (VCs), but the majority of technical start-ups will require investment from VCs in order to scale their business globally. Start-up and accelerator programmes provide one route to VCs. Another route is through industry experts such as David Tighe, head of innovation for the Bank of Ireland. Alternatively, you can approach the VCs directly. Just ask.

Interview with David Tighe, Head of Innovation for the Bank of Ireland

David Tighe's role is focused on where the bank is going, what the core changes in technology happening for their customers are and how fintech (finance and technology) and start-ups are affecting the future of the banks.

What support does Bank of Ireland (BOI) Innovation offer start-ups?

When a start-up comes to us, we look at the product and the process and the business that they are developing, and how that can engage and work with Bank of Ireland. We talk to start-ups at every level of the business, from the initial 'bedroom' idea all the way through to where you are looking to grow. We look at different models that can support them, through mentorship, advice or funding. We can refer to venture capital, or, from a lending perspective, we can refer to our own business banking channel.

I have a team of people working with me: an entrepreneur in residence, two community managers and three insight and innovation managers. We have recently opened up workbenches at branches in Grand Canal Square, Dublin, and Mainguard Street, Galway. A workbench is a drop-in space – a co-working space with free Wi-Fi, tea and coffee. We also recently launched the Start-Up Lab in Eyre Square, Galway, a tech incubator there which is the first of its kind. Up to six start-up teams will be selected and BOI Innovation will work with them in the lab for six months on areas such as mentorship, pitching, on the business itself and accelerating the business through providing access to venture capitalists. We will work to roll out more workbenches throughout the country.

The most important thing that we can tell people is whether or not we believe the idea will work. One of the key things is to let businesses understand how we see them. There is no point in saying, 'Yes, your business is successful, it's going to do really well,' and then not responding and not engaging.

It is really important that every engagement that we have is honest and credible. We are there to support what they are doing. Everything we do at the workbenches will be based on transparency, to provide better advice and guidance.

Do start-ups pitch to BOI Innovation?

Any engagement with BOI Innovation is a pitch, however, it is not just about pitching to us for funds. BOI Innovation does not specifically provide funding. We link to the venture capitalists, we link to our own lending fund and we link to other partners. Between each other, we engage and manage that ecosystem.

In my role as head of innovation, I get ten to fifteen pitches a week, concerning different businesses and what they are doing, and how Bank of Ireland might purchase that product or partner with that business to put out something new to our customers.

A scheduled pitch from a start-up would always be made in a face-to-face meeting, and most often within a one-hour meeting. You may get a lot of good guys, hustling really well. They might grab me at the workbench or meet me at a conference that I am speaking at and then give me a quick, two-minute pitch to spark my interest and bring me in.

How important is the elevator pitch?

The elevator pitch is hugely important. It should pique the interest and set a good tone for what that business is about. If you get it wrong, it can cripple you, but a good two-minute elevator pitch can open up interest from any area.

What happens in a scheduled pitch?

In a scheduled meeting, we normally ask businesses to pitch for no more than ten minutes. Anything longer than that does not do service to the business. We generally have a pitch or presentation around the business, and then I'll do a Q&A with them. You can get everything you need from a half-hour to forty-minute conversation.

Do you like the use of slides in a pitch?

I have no issue with slides being used in a pitch, but if they use them they should aid their story, not be their story. I run a mile from anything that is not PowerPoint – I just do not get Prezi. Images are very important to help your words, but your words are the most important.

What content do you look for in a pitch?

We get a range of pitches, from working out the kinks in the business to very polished pitches with a clear understanding of what they are doing and where they are going. I am always keen to find out who is on the team – it is just as important as your product. The pitch needs to highlight the qualifications, skills and expertise within the team. The one thing that turns me off the most in a pitch is diving into the complexities of the business.

In terms of content, addressing the problem, solution, market, team and financials is all important, but be realistic about what all five are. I find it jarring (even pointless, at times) to hear, 'The potential market is five billion in the health market in the world, but we're only going after a small cohort in the Irish market and we're going to take ten percent of it.' Be realistic about what you are actually going after.

Are you looking for a good idea or a good team, or both?

If you can find a really credible team, you can sometimes recommend them based not on the idea, but what they are going to achieve as a team no matter what they do. I am looking for a really well-thought-out understanding of the problem, the affected market and how they are going to answer the customer's problem, as well as a good team to develop it.

How important is the style of delivery in a pitch?

The delivery style of the pitch is hugely important. I say this to everybody I talk to. It is important in my own presentations, when I am talking to people within the bank and outside the bank. Tone and inflection are hugely important. I have seen, in pitches, how people can be extremely enthusiastic and passionate about their business, but how that all falls away if they are not changing the tone, and enhancing and using different inflections in their speech.

How important is the start-up story?

One of the things that I have always championed is the role of the storyteller within the team, and their ability to tell the story of what they are doing and where they are going clearly, concisely and engagingly. It cannot be underestimated that the story will actually be fundamental to any success for your business.

What mistakes do start-ups make in a pitch?

Start-ups think we are hugely excited by the technical detail, but in the early stages this is not necessarily the case. We need to know the problem you are solving, what market you are going after, who the customers are – and whether you have talked to and verified them – and who the team is. The technology will come later. At that very early stage, the key is to be able to tell that story, at a high level, with the potential in your pocket.

What the Venture Capitalists Say

Before a meeting with a venture capitalist, do your research and find out what types of companies they have already invested in. Contact one or more of those companies, and see if they can offer you any advice ahead of your meeting. Make sure you know the duration of the meeting, and what the format is – be it a ten-minute presentation or twenty-minute Q&A. Do they expect slides? If so, how many, and should you send them in beforehand?

Interview with Seán O'Sullivan, Founder of SOSventures

SOSventures has its headquarters in Cork and offices in the US and China. I had the pleasure of working with Seán when he appeared as a 'Dragon' on series three and four of 'Dragons' Den'.

What investment does SOSventures provide to start-ups?

SOSventures primarily invest through companies we fund via accelerator programs that we run, from selr8r to haxlr8r to synbio. Initial funding of $25,000 to $50,000 is typical for the first three months. Our top investments top out at $2 million or so per round of financing.

What content needs to be covered in a pitch?

Product, market, team and customer traction are of almost equal importance in a pitch, but if the team is not strong enough, flexible enough and fun enough to work with for the next seven years, that will kill it.

How important is delivery style?

Delivery style in a pitch is very important. I prefer Keynote to PowerPoint or Prezi, although start-ups often pitch without using slides.

What are the main mistakes that start-ups make?

The main mistake that start-ups make is 'losing the forest for the trees': caring too much about the financials and not enough about the customer's needs, or making up a business model that only suits the business, but does not make sense for the customer.

What advice can you give start-ups?

Settle in for a wild ride. The average start-up takes seven years before any success can be achieved, and it is not uncommon for it to take ten or twelve years. Enjoy what you do every day, and do what you do honourably and sustainably, because it is going to take a while for you to build something really, really great.

What does a start-up need to apply for seed investment with SOSventures?

To apply for seed investment with SOSventures, you need to be better than the other ninety-five percent that apply.

Interview with Bill Liao, European Venture Partner With SOSventures and Co-Founder of CoderDojo

Bill Liao is a serial entrepreneur, and a social entrepreneur. His tips on pitching are on his website www.makeitcrisp.com. I met Bill working with the synbio axlr8r in Cork.

How should you prepare for an investment pitch?

- Make your pitch crisp, and totally authentic.
- Practise it on strangers at least one hundred times.
- Make sure you have a clear story.
- Fill it with memorable sound bites.
- Make sure that your story makes your potential investors feel smarter.

What, in your view, should make up the content of a pitch?

- Purpose
- Problem
- Credibility
- Solution

- Team
- Market
- Financials

How should a pitch be delivered?

The pitch should be delivered by the CEO as a clear story, with minimal visuals emphasising clear points.

How important is the story?

How important is oxygen? The story must be authentic, clear, credible, simple and surprising, and have a happy ending.

Interview with Eamonn Quinn, Investment Analyst and Chairman, Kelsius

I had the pleasure of working with Eamonn when he was a 'Dragon' on the sixth series of 'Dragons' Den'.

What, in your view, should be in a pitch?

Pitching is about two things: the pitcher and the pitch. Does the pitcher really believe the story and do they have the experience to back it up? They will have to inspire other people to come along the journey with them. Initially, the pitch should be delivered without any props, as if you were meeting someone for coffee or in a pub. After that, a few props or a demo can certainly add weight or make the idea come alive.

Practise your elevator pitch and really figure out a way to quickly explain what the idea is, then use the rest of the time explaining why you think it will work.

You can often spend five minutes listening to an investment pitch and still not have grasped what they are trying to achieve. The mind, I will be honest, starts to wander.

In my experience, all financials look identical in terms of sales and growth, but you still need them, and you need to know the costs, margins and the competitive set in the market place.

Interview with George Zachary, Venture Capitalist, Charles River Ventures (CRV)

CRV manage a fund of approximately $1.4 billion, and bought one percent of Twitter in 2006 – almost as soon as the company was born – for $250,000. George was part of the judging panel for 'Entrepreneur Idol' in Stanford Business School in 2008. I contacted him for an interview, and he was delighted to share his insights.

What do you expect in an investment pitch?

I allocate a maximum of one hour to investment pitches, but I need to be impressed within the first ten minutes. I like people to send me their slides in advance, which helps me understand what they are doing so that we can have a more productive first meeting. It also helps me screen out companies that have zero possibility of funding. I prefer simple slides, so PowerPoint is better – Prezi is too distracting.

The focus should be on the founder, and their company and products, not on special effects in the presentation software. We ask for no more than twenty slides to make their pitch, but they can bring extra slides as backup for questions that may get asked.

I have also seen how slides can hinder a pitch. When the founder speaks from their mind and heart, the slides come off well. If a founder just reads the slides it comes across as weak. In general, slides should be a supporting medium for the founder and their pitch.

The main mistake that start-ups make is not being clear enough about what the product is, what it does and why a great business can be built. It is not just about creating a great revenue line, but about a profitable business that also changes the world.

Interview with Orla Rimmington, Partner with Kernel Capital

Kernel Capital is a venture capital firm with offices in Cork, Dublin and Belfast.

What is Kernel Capital?

Established in 1999, Kernel Capital is the independent manager of the Bank of Ireland Kernel Capital Venture Funds, one of the largest and most active sources of equity finance for technology companies on the island of Ireland. Kernel Capital is regulated by the Central Bank of Ireland.

What are the main criteria for a start-up to apply for funding with Kernel Capital?

We target promoters who are honest, intelligent and capable, and have a strong work ethic, primarily but not exclusively from within the information and communications technology (ICT) and engineering sectors. We invest where the company promoters can demonstrate their deep understanding of the market opportunity, and how they will create novel products enabling international sales of scale.

Does the start-up have to match the funding?

No, we are more focused on the calibre of the promoters, their industry relationships and their networks rather than on any matching funding requirement. In general, the Bank of Ireland Kernel Capital Venture Funds is the lead investor; we complete our own due diligence and investment analysis on all opportunities. Although we frequently co-invest, we do not require investment by others to justify our decisions.

What is the range of funding that KernelCapital offers a start-up?

We target companies in which we can ultimately invest €2 million to €5 million. We do not have a minimum investment threshold, and we have made multiple investments in young companies in the range of €100,000 to €500,000, with subsequent substantial follow-on funding.

How many people would normally sit on the panel for funding?

At least two partners from our team of six full-time partners at Kernel Capital will have had a number of meetings with the prospective investee, and advocate for the investment. All six partners will be well-read on the proposal and related due diligence. Ultimately, the investment decision will be taken by the full team.

How long are the meetings?

The initial meetings may be informal, over coffee. We then follow with more structured meetings with a defined agenda, which are approximately 1.5 to three hours.

How many meetings would you have before making a decision?

After the introductory, informal meetings, two structured meetings will generally follow. In between these meetings we do our own in-depth due diligence on all aspects of the opportunity.

Who would typically make up the panel?

The panel is comprised of at least of two partners and other investment committee executives, with all partners being fully appraised of the opportunity.

At what stage should a start-up be at in order to apply for funding from Kernel Capital?

It is never too early to create awareness of your company and to gain constructive feedback on your value proposition. At our Kernel Capital 'Open Hours' events, we meet with entrepreneurs throughout the country in an informal setting to determine if they would be a good future match for Kernel Capital, and vice versa. We have backed ideas and concepts even before the start-up was formally incorporated. When we approached Professor Mark Davies and Dr Tara Dalton at the University of Limerick, they had world-class technology, but were yet to form a company. We initially backed them with €100,000, then invested €1.8 million, and their company, Stokes Bio Ltd, went on to sell for $44 million to NASDAQ-quoted Life Technologies. Similarly, when Cathal McGloin and Mícheál Ó Foghlú of FeedHenry, Waterford, came to see us we provided their first venture capital funding of €500,000. We then invested a further €2 million; the company was later acquired by Red Hat Incorporated for $82 million.

What is the calibre of the pitches you see?

The pitches we see are generally good, as we work to ensure that, prior to approaching us, entrepreneurs know what our investment sweet spot is. We receive around 300 pitches annually, and make about fifteen new and fifteen 'follow-on' investments a year. For us, if a promoter demonstrates integrity, vision and a strong work ethic, we are not too concerned with how slick or otherwise their pitch may be. It is important to remember that Apple, Google, Facebook and many other great companies were founded by young entrepreneurs, with no previous start-up or pitching experience. If one ruled out those who may not pitch well, you would be leaving many great opportunities behind.

What content do you expect in a pitch, and in what order?

When pitching in a formal setting, entrepreneurs should, firstly, clearly articulate the opportunity they are addressing and their value proposition. It is important to us that they focus on key areas such as product or technology differentiation and defencibility, and demonstrate how and why their offering can beat the competition.

During their pitch, promoters should tell us the story of their company, and bring across their vision for the business and how they will execute it. A pitch should ideally include a demo of the actual product or service. Where appropriate, pitches should also provide a clear description of the business model, and establish the position in the supply chain that the product or service fits. It is okay if this has not yet been fully worked out, just as long as they are aware of the challenges. Indeed, for many 'platform technologies' it may not even be appropriate to have a rigidly defined business model and path-to-market at an early stage. Being transparent is key – we appreciate honesty from the outset. We have first-hand experience of the challenges and opportunities that early-stage companies face. We expect entrepreneurs presenting business strengths, then adding credibility by pointing out weaknesses and presenting planned solutions.

As pitches are not always formal, it is important to have your elevator pitch ready for any brief, opportune encounters. A couple of years ago at an InterTradeIreland event we heard a promoter casually advise that, through his former employer, he was the named inventor on a patented technology that was used in almost half of the DVD players manufactured in the world. Through our own network, we verified this claim, and the technical and visionary skills of the promoter, Tim Cummins. We subsequently gave him an initial €100,000 to incorporate his new start-up, ChipSensors, followed by a further €1.8 million investment. The company was successfully sold in 2010 to NASDAQ-quoted Silicon Laboratories, returning a thirty-three percent IRR (internal rate of return). In 2014, we invested in Tim's new company, Altratech.

Do you invest in the idea, the person or both?

At Kernel Capital, first and foremost, it is about people. We have had many successes where we have collaborated with the promoters to progressively evolve the company's idea. In fact, we do this quite often. The key is to find intelligent individuals with vision, capable of building the right team over the right time period; it does not have to happen all at once. We fund companies through this period to deliver momentum and scale. We support and assist promoters as they build their teams, but changing the promoters is not for us.

How important is delivery style in a pitch?

There is no doubt that good posture, facial expression, voice projection and strong eye contact can aid effective pitch delivery. However, we are firm believers that these attributes do not come naturally to everyone. We want entrepreneurs to be themselves; we want to meet genuine people, not false personas.

Do you prefer PowerPoint, Keynote or Prezi?

It is less about how the presentation looks, and more about the content of the presentation. My advice to entrepreneurs is to use a medium that they are comfortable with.

Do start-ups ever pitch to you without slides?

Yes, and they have been some of the best and most memorable pitches we have received. Regardless of the medium, a basic piece of advice is that entrepreneurs should always speak in a language that investors will understand, avoiding terminology that the promoter has invented and resisting the temptation to overload potential investors with industry data rather than the key relevant information. The goal at a first pitch is to secure our interest, such that we are the party who are most keen to follow up.

How important is the start-up story?

For Kernel Capital, the story of how the promoters got to be where they are is incredibly important. An unconvincing story leaves credibility gaps, and can make or break an investor pitch. A start-up with no story to tell often lacks direction. Entrepreneurs should never underestimate the importance of the story that lies behind their idea. Often overlooked as irrelevant, the founding story can really captivate investors, employees and customers, and encapsulates the true essence of the company.

What are the main mistakes that start-ups make in a pitch?

The most common is the most basic – lack of preparation. Entrepreneurs are often so focused on their pitch that they neglect to research the party to whom they are presenting. Before approaching us, a promoter should research our firm, and whom he or she is presenting to. Why is their pitch likely to be attractive to us? Do we have the skill sets, network and track record applicable to the proposed investment? Aspiring entrepreneurs should target investors with a strong, relevant track record, and ensure that their funding needs are in line with their respective strategies. It is really important that a company seeking investment secures the right investor. We do not invest in every good opportunity we see, as we only invest where we know we can add value. We have built our portfolio in keeping with this approach.

What tips or advice would you give to start-ups regarding their pitch?

There is no one right way to pitch to a venture capitalist, however integrity always wins out. All entrepreneurs have unique skills and talents to offer, some verbalise well, while others write well or have particular strengths with numbers, some can sell and others can invent. We appreciate that it takes different kinds of minds and a healthy mix of strengths and talent to make a world-class team. With this in mind, my best advice to any entrepreneur seeking investment is to be yourself, and be honest. Try to put yourself in our position, and address the questions we will be seeking answers to. We do not expect promoters to have all the answers immediately, yet it is important to have an appreciation of the relevance of the questions. If there is one thing I cannot stress enough, it is the importance of focused preparation for the specific engagement. As the great inventor Alexander Graham Bell once said: 'Before anything else, preparation is the key to success.'

Chapter Eight

AUDIENCE AND CONTENT

The content of your pitch will be determined by who your audience is. The key is to research your audience as best you can beforehand. You have seen in some of the interviews up to now, that even within a certain category of people – accelerator programme directors or venture capitalists, for example, people have different views and opinions. At least having thought about your audience beforehand and why they should care about what you are going to say, you have a better chance of engaging them.

Audience Questionnaire

1. Who is in your audience?

2. What are their roles, responsibilities and interests?

3. How will they benefit from hearing what you have to say?

4. What do they already know about the topic?

5. What are three things this audience needs to know about you?

6. How can you emotionally connect with this audience?

7. What would you like this audience to do, think or feel as a result of what you have to say?

8. What questions do you think your audience might ask?

9. How do you think your audience will react?

10. How would you like your audience to react? Visualise it!

It is useful jotting down the answers to at least some of these questions, and making a note of anything else that comes to mind about the audience you will be speaking to. It is also worthwhile talking through your answers with someone. It is not enough to have the answers in your head – putting pen to paper helps clarify your thoughts even further. You can then take it one step further by verbalising your answers and getting feedback from a friend, family member or colleague willing to give you a few minutes of their time. They might remark upon something you had not yet thought of.

Creative brainstorming and structuring content

Once you are clear about your target audience, it is time to start thinking about your content. In order to think from the heart, I urge you to tap into your creativity while brainstorming.

Brainstorming is just about jotting down words and ideas that come to mind when thinking about a certain topic. In this case, you are brainstorming ideas about what content you should include in your pitch, presentation or speech. Instead of using full sentences, try to jot down keywords, being as bold and creative as you like. It is a method of idea generation, and there is no right or wrong; anything goes. You may end up using some of what you note down, none of it or all of it.

One method I use in my workshops, to prepare for a brainstorming session, is a two-minute mindful-breathing meditation. I have used it with hundreds of senior executives, managers and entrepreneurs. It helps to clear the mind and allows people to pause their thoughts, parking any preconceptions about what they think should be in the pitch, presentation or speech. Then they can start brainstorming with a blank slate. After a short mindful-breathing meditation, we can think more calmly and clearly.

I use a two-minute mindful-breathing meditation adapted from Sam Young's *Guided Mindfulness Meditations*. Sam is a good friend as well as a teacher of mindfulness, and he kindly gave me permission to edit his meditation for the purpose of my workshop. Sam based his meditations on the work of Eckhart Tolle and *The Power of Now*.

Sam Young's mindful-breathing meditation

Begin by finding a comfortable and stable posture.

Check that you are sitting upright.

Your back should be straight, but not rigid: shoulders loose, head erect and balanced, face soft and body still.

Sit with your back away from the chair, so that your spine is self-supporting.

Place your feet flat on the floor.

Gently close your eyes.

And now become aware of your body.

How does it feel? Is it tense, or relaxed?

Scan your body gently from head to foot.

And now, become aware of the fact that you are breathing.

Sense or feel how you experience your breath.

Perhaps there is coolness in your nose, or the back of your throat.

Or movement in your chest.

Or the rise and fall of your abdomen.

Become aware of the movement of your breath as it enters your body, and as it leaves your body.

Become aware of your breath in your body.

Do not think about it, just feel it, experience it.

The most healing place to feel your breath is in your abdomen – your belly.

Feel the movement in your abdomen as you breathe.

Feel the expansion of your abdomen as you breathe in, and the contraction of your abdomen as you breathe out.

If you are having difficulty feeling the movement in your abdomen, it might be helpful to take slightly deeper, fuller breaths, without straining, so that the expansion and contraction in your abdomen is more perceptible.

Feel each breath as it comes in, and goes out.

Feel your abdomen gently expanding and contracting.

Simply be here in each moment, with each breath.

Do not try to do anything. Do not try to get anywhere.

Simply be with yourself and your breathing.

As you focus your attention on your breath, you will notice, from time to time, that your mind has wandered. This is normal.

Do not judge yourself when this happens.

Instead, each time that you notice your attention is no longer on your breath, gently bring it back to experiencing your breath in your body.

Experience the movement, Experience the sensations.

Give your full attention to each breath in, to each breath out.

As you feel your breath, try not to control it. Let it find its own rhythm.

Just be aware of each breath in, and each breath out.

Notice where your attention is right now.

If it is not on your breath, then gently bring it back to experiencing your breath.

Do not control or interfere with it in any way.

Whenever you notice that you are not present with your breath, not feeling it, gently bring your attention back to experiencing your breath in your body.

Stay with your breath. Be acutely aware of what it feels like to breathe.

Be aware of the sensations and the movements that it is creating in your body, at this moment.

As you breathe, feel your body expanding, then feel your body contracting.

Feel the sensations in your body as you breathe in, then feel the sensations in your body as you breathe out.

Observe the flow of your breathing, moment by moment.

Be fully present. Stay with your breath. Feel it.

Your in breath. Your out breath.

Now that we have paused our thoughts for a few minutes through the breath meditation, we can start brainstorming, with a blank slate. This pausing of one's thought acts in the same way as the white space around a piece of text, helping you to think more clearly, in the same way that the white space helps you to see the text more clearly.

Colour

As part of my workshop, I then place a blank piece of paper and some coloured markers in front of each participant. I encourage them to use colours while brainstorming content, as this helps to tap into the right side of the brain – the more creative side –

enabling them to think from the heart, and draw upon their emotions. While Tony Buzan uses colour as part of his famous mind-mapping technique, I'm not suggesting that you mind-map here – I just think that it is useful to write keywords in different colours. Once people start using colours while brainstorming, they sometimes start drawing images. This could also be a way of remembering the points you want to make, if you associate colours or images with keywords.

Music

During the workshop I play a piece of music in the background while the group is brainstorming. It lasts for about four minutes. My favourite music to use in the workshop is a piece called 'Life' by an Italian composer called Ludovico Einaudi, from his album *In a Time Lapse*. I have also used music by the British composer, Rachel Portman. Choose any piece of music that you find relaxes you.

I have always believed that music elevates the mind and helps us to think on a different frequency. It turns out that I'm not wrong.

I recently met a girl during a corporate training session I was giving on 'Presenting with Impact'. She opted to do a presentation on something outside of work – on the Japanese author, researcher and entrepreneur, Dr Masaru Emoto, who passed away in 2014. Dr Emoto carried out numerous studies on the transformative effects of beautiful classical music on water crystals. Considering that our bodies are sixty percent water, it is no wonder that this type of music also transforms our thinking.

Quick Recap

After you have finished brainstorming, take a look at what you have on the page in front of you and see if there is anything different to what you would normally put in your pitch, presentation or speech. Did any new ideas come to mind? A way of connecting emotionally with your target audience, perhaps? Do not worry if this is not the case – it is still early days. After the brainstorming session, look over any other notes you may have, and add any important keywords that you may have left out.

Carving the content into a story

You have spent weeks – maybe months – gathering all your information. Now, you have to start carving. Think of a sculpture: the artist has a block of stone and must chip away at the stone and put some shape onto it. It is similar to your pitch, presentation or speech. It is similar, even, to this book, which in itself is a large presentation.

I carried out many interviews, all of which I wanted to use. I couldn't. I tried, but it didn't work. So I took my own advice: instead of using a two-minute mindful-breathing meditation, I went away for three days. No training. No school lunches. No pick-ups. No television. No Wi-Fi. I went to a deserted town that looked like something out of an Alfred Hitchcock movie: just a beautiful beach, blue sky and cool, fresh air. On my breaks from writing, I walked the beach. I had to clear my head, see things from a different perspective, simplify my message and start carving. Back in my room, I had my colours with me, and I had some of my favourite music on my laptop. The creative side of my brain started to kick in. I started to see some shape the night before leaving. I could see the wood from the trees, as it were. The story was finally starting to come through, after six months of work, and one week to go before the deadline.

The recipe

After completing your creative brainstorming, we can look at the 'recipe' for crafting a pitch, presentation or speech. I said at the start of this book that pitching is an art, not a science, and there is no magic formula. Nevertheless, people have time pressures and everything is easier with a formula, template or recipe.

I am calling it a recipe because, as with any recipe, you can make it your own by adding ingredients or leaving a few out as you go along.

You cannot use all of the information you have on your topic in your pitch, presentation or speech; you must pick the golden nuggets for your particular audience. That is not to say that the rest of the information goes to waste. I once read that a presentation should be two percent of the information, with ninety-eight-percent reserved for the questions and answers afterwards. This may be a little extreme, but remember that less is often more.

Start by writing one sentence outlining the message you want your audience to take away from this pitch, presentation or speech.

For example:

- To an audience of investors: I want to convince them that this product will change the world.

- To an audience of new mothers: I want to persuade them that their babies will love my new organic baby food.

- To an audience of senior management: I want to inform them that these cuts will have a serious impact on our department.

This one-line takeaway message is the measure of your success. At the end of your pitch, presentation or speech you can ask yourself, 'Did I convince those investors?', 'Did I persuade that audience of mothers?' or 'Did I inform senior management of the serious impact?'

Having that one-line takeaway message clear in your mind will help to keep you on track. If, halfway through your pitch, you begin to go off on a tangent, your takeaway message will help to bring you back.

What's the story?

Your overall pitch, presentation or speech needs to be simple, engaging and memorable. It needs to tell a story.

From here on in, I am going to refer to your pitch, presentation or speech as your 'story'. You need to think of a 'wow' opening. This is probably the most important part. If you do not grab the attention of your audience in the first few seconds, it will be very difficult to get their attention later on.

I was always mindful of this when writing feature articles for the *Irish Independent*. If I cannot capture a reader's attention in the opening paragraph they will flick through and begin reading the next article. I find my own tolerance can wane when reading a new book that does not grab my attention in the first page or two. Why would I waste my time reading something that does not interest me?

Wow opening

The opening needs to have the audience sitting up in their seats, thinking, 'This sounds interesting. I'll listen to this one.' The alternative is, 'Oh no, another boring presentation. I wonder what I'll have for lunch.'

Your wow opening could be a quote, a question, a bold fact, figure or statement, a reference to something you heard on the radio or read in the newspaper or a book. Choose something interesting that is relevant to what you are going to talk about, something that gives your audience a reason to care.

Main body

Your opening should then lead on to your first point. There needs to be a logical flow to your story, where A leads to B, then B leads to C. You should take the audience by the hand, step by step, throughout your story, which must have a beginning, a middle and an end. I would suggest using between three and five umbrella headings as your main points. It works best if you can limit it to three.

There must be a smooth transition between your points. You do not always have to say it, but it should be implied. There needs to be an invisible line between each point: 'This leads me to . . . ' If you do not have this transition, it can be difficult for the audience to follow your train of thought. It must be easy for the audience to follow what it is that you are saying.

A pitch for investment could fall under five headings: problem, solution, market, team and financials. There is a logical progression here that you can fit your unique story around: the problem you came across and where you were or what you were doing at the time; the solution you came up with, different to anything else available; the market, and research done on the size of the market, target market and route to market; the team you have working with you, advising you or who you plan to hire; and financials, so, what money you need, what you are going to do with it and how you are going to make money from this idea, product or service.

Closing

You need to finish your story with a strong ending. Do not leave it hanging in mid-air. Include a brief summary of what you have spoken about, thank the audience for listening and establish a course of action for the future. The closing should overlap with the opening, and the story should be brought full circle. Refer back to whatever you opened with – be it a quote, question, fact, figure, statement or reference. I have used this technique in articles and seen other feature journalists use it. I have also heard it used in talks and seminars, where it works to add a sense of completion to the presentation, similar to the way in which 'The End' works at the end of a movie: you know it is over, and so does the audience.

You need to get the story right before even thinking of slides. You also need to be able to tell the same story in many different ways, not just learn it off by heart. Your story should be structured in such a way that it rolls off your tongue as easily as if you were talking about a rugby match you were at last Saturday, or a concert you attended. You could meet ten different people, and tell the same story ten different ways. It would not necessarily be told exactly the same way each time, but the essential content of the story would be the same – the same beginning, middle and end, and the same characters and plot.

One thing to remember is that your story will be ever-changing. New information will need to be added, and old information will need to be removed. You need to be fluent and flexible, not reliant on having to say it in one particular way. The more often you practise, the more familiar you will be with the material and the more fluent you will in turn become.

Try to outline your story with five keywords, perhaps a keyword for each of your five umbrella headings, or a keyword for your opening, another for the three main points and a final keyword for the closing. I suggest that you build a sound bite around each keyword. A sound bite is a short sentence or phrase that is easy to remember, often included in a speech or interview and repeated in the media. It should capture the essence of your point in a few short words.

Keywords and sound bites

If I were to use three keywords and sound bites to build on my workshop, they would be the following:

Keyword 1: Audience

Sound bite: The starting point of any pitch is your audience.

Keyword 2: Content

Sound bite: Think of the content of your pitch in terms of a story.

Keyword 3: Delivery

Sound bite: Delivery plays a huge part in the impact of your message.

Regardless of how long or short my workshop is, I build it around those three keywords and sound bites.

I have provided space on the next few pages for a sample worksheet I use in my 'Perfect Pitch' workshop.

Structuring the Content of Your Story: A Recipe for Success

Goals of the Pitch

What message do you want the audience to take away?

What do you want the audience to do, think or feel as a result of your takeaway message?

Opening of the Pitch

What's your wow opening? (A statement, problem, idea, quotation or question.)

```



```

Body of the Pitch: First Point

What's the first point you want to make?

```



```

Write down the background research you have to support that first point. For example, an anecdote, a case study, personal experience, facts or statistics.

```



```

What logical link will you use to transition to your second point ('This leads me to . . . ')?

```



```

Body of the Pitch: Second Point

What's the second point you want to make?

Write down the background research you have to support that second point. For example, an anecdote, a case study, personal experience, facts or statistics.

What logical link will you use to transition to your third point ('This leads me to . . . ')?

Body of the Pitch: Third Point

What's the third point you want to make?

Write down the background research you have to support that third point. For example, an anecdote, a case study, personal experience, facts or statistics.

What logical link will you use to transition to your fourth point, if you're going to include on ('This leads me to . . . ')?

Body of the Pitch: Additional Points

Feel free to add fourth, fifth and additional points as needed.

Closing the Pitch

Include a summary of your main points, an overlap with your opening, a thank you for listening and action for the future, for example, opening the floor to questions or meeting afterwards for further discussion.

Naomi Fein, Founder of Think Visual

The executive director of the Dublin City University Innovation Campus asked me to deliver a pitch workshop at the Beef Hackathon in March 2015. There was going to be €10,000 as the first prize, so they were anticipating that some 'serious entrepreneurs' would be in attendance. It was a weekend event, and the presentations on the Sunday were going to be made to senior government officials, as well as to corporate leaders from IBM, Intel and ABP Foods. What I did not know was that Naomi Fein, founder of Think Visual, was going to be sitting in the back row harvesting my workshop. Naomi and her team were also working at the Beef Hackathon that weekend, and had seen my workshop advertised and decided to sit in. Naomi introduced herself to me afterwards and showed me her visuals. I was amazed by how she had captured the essence of my message in such a short space of time. I have included these visuals at the end of this chapter, and in the next chapter on delivery.

Naomi and I had both heard about each other's work through Wayne Murphy prior to that weekend. Wayne had seen both of our work separately in the Bank of Ireland Accelerator Programme, and he thought that we should meet up. Naomi and I have since worked together on some successful joint projects. Naomi says:

> We listen to complex information (at conferences, events, workshops, meetings, one-on-one) and we 'harvest' the complex knowledge and re-tell it. Because we are visual creatures, we use visual, storyful language which makes it more memorable, actionable and shareable.

In order to make beautiful graphic harvests, you need to start with a great story. When you have the story, the visuals just appear in our heads. Once they are in our heads, it's an easy journey to put them on the screen.

Graphic harvesting done by Naomi Fein, founder of Think Visual.

Chapter Nine

DELIVERY

The delivery of your pitch, presentation or speech can be divided into three main elements: the content or words that you use, your voice and your body language.

Words

Your choice of words and language is very important. Ensure that the words you use are as positive as possible, and avoid words that imply uncertainty, such as 'try', 'might', 'may', 'maybe', 'hope' or 'should'. Replace them with more definite words like 'can' and 'will'. I find that it is best to use colloquial language and a conversational tone – imagine that you are having a cup of tea and a chat with a friend.

Voice

The last thing you want is to sound monotonous, so vary the use of pitch, pace, pause and pressure when speaking. The voice is like a musical instrument; it can be played in many different ways with variations in tone, volume and pace. The voice is key to engaging your audience and bringing your topic to life.

Variation of pitch

Within your voice you have high, middle and low pitches, and a range of inflections in between. If you remain within the one pitch, your voice will come across as monotonous – it is up to you to vary the pitch of your voice. If, for example, you were talking about something serious, you might lower your pitch. Alternatively, if you were excited about something, your pitch would be higher.

When moving on to a new sentence, raise your voice to a higher pitch at the opening. Similarly, raise the pitch of your voice when you are moving on to talk about something new. It is a great indicator to the audience that you have finished one point and you are now moving on to a new point.

Variation of pace

Another way of varying your voice is through your use of pace. You may want to speed up when talking about a subject that you think the audience is familiar with, or slow down if you are talking about something more complex. However, it is important to remember that we all tend to speak a little faster when we are nervous. We therefore need to make a conscious effort to slow down when speaking in front of a group. You do not want to give the impression that you want to get it over with as quickly as possible, and the audience will find it difficult keeping up with people who speak too fast – you need to make it easy for them to grasp what you are talking about. If they miss any words, they may lose the thread of your message and switch off.

Pressure

You can vary your voice by adding emphasis to important words in a sentence. This helps certain words stand out. Perhaps there is a keyword that you want to highlight. For example, 'The *problem* people face', or 'The *solution* we have come up with'. By adding extra emphasis on that word, you are ensuring that people receive the core message you are trying to get across.

I have noticed that people tend to put a keyword at the end of sentences and not only not emphasise them, but actually lower the pitch of their voice so much that they cannot be heard, resulting in the entire message being lost.

In addition to emphasising keywords, you need to ensure that you project your voice so that people can actually hear what you are saying. Judge the size of the room and its acoustics. If you cannot be heard, you are wasting your time and everyone else's. If the people in the back row cannot hear you, they will become restless, which can have a ripple effect, and cause unease within the room. To be as inclusive as possible you need to ensure that the lady in the last row on the far right who is hard of hearing can hear and understand what you are saying. She could be the one with the money.

Pause

It is of huge importance knowing when to pause, as it helps with the rhythm of the sentence. Pausing allows the audience to take in what you have just said, and gives you time to think about what you are going to say next. You can combine pause with emphasis to create a dramatic pause before or after a keyword that you have just emphasised, to drive home your message. For example, '*Ninety-five percent* (pause) of people who bought our product said they would buy it again.' Rhetorical questions are a great way to draw in an audience when speaking. Make sure that you pause for a split second after the use of a rhetorical question. This is called a rhetorical pause. 'So, where do we do we go from here? (pause)' for example, gives the audience time to think. Obviously do not pause for too long, or someone from the audience may decide to answer your question. A split-second pause is enough to get people thinking.

In Ireland, we have a lot of what are called 'gap fillers'. We are afraid of the silence provided by a pause. Instead of pausing, we tend to fill the gaps with 'Ehm', 'You know', 'I suppose' and so on. Your audience will eventually start counting the number of times you say 'I suppose' instead of listening to what you are saying. Avoid this distraction by simply pausing.

Body language

It is worth thinking about your body language. Watch people delivering a message, and see who has the most impact for you. Note their posture, stance, movements and gestures. Then compare them with someone else who has had less of an impact. Does their body language have anything to do with the impact of their presentation?

Going back a number of years to when I was judging presentations on a third-year marketing programme in UCD, I remember the two students I gave full marks to, both only about nineteen years of age. I asked them how they had managed to deliver such excellent presentations and, in response, they said they had studied Steve Jobs, the former Apple CEO.

Jobs passed away in 2011, but his presentations are still on YouTube. The introduction of the iPhone in 2007 is a great example of him and his stage presence. A pitch or presentation is like a stage performance: your posture, movement and gestures are your stage presence. Command the floor in the same way that an actor commands the stage.

Posture

Let me start with posture. The person who stands tall – shoulders back, with their feet almost glued to the floor – is perceived as being confident. I use the word 'perceived', because you may not be confident, but your stance allows you to be perceived as such. How you are perceived, and the first impression you give, are important. As the saying goes, 'You never get a second chance to make a first impression.' When presenting, you need to look confident to instil confidence in your audience. There is a great TED Talk by Amy Cuddy called 'Your Body Language Shapes Who You Are'. Amy is a social psychologist, and has researched how 'power posing' – standing in a confident posture, even when we do not feel confident – can affect testosterone and cortisol levels in the brain, and might even have an impact on our chances for success. You may not have started off feeling confident, but if you act confident by adopting a confident posture, it will help you to begin to feel confident. Fake it until you become it.

If you have a habit of slouching, try the following exercise. Walk to the nearest wall with a flat surface without grooves or pictures. Align your heels with the bottom of the wall or skirting board, then place the base of your spine against the wall. Slowly roll your spine against the wall until your shoulders are also touching the wall. Step away from the wall, give your body a little shake and then take a few steps forward. Do you feel taller? Do you feel more confident?

Movement

It is fine moving around the floor when presenting in front of an audience, but I think a controlled movement is better than shuffling from side to side or back and forth. I have seen people practically dancing around the floor during a pitch, while others have paced up and down. These random movements can be distracting to the audience, and can also be perceived as a sign of nerves. If you want to move, pick a point on the floor, move there and then glue your feet to the floor again. This makes it less distracting for your audience. It can be useful moving to a different spot as you transition from one point to another. It can also be an indicator to your audience that you are moving on to a new point.

Gestures

So, you are now standing tall, with a confident posture and not moving around too much. Now, what do you do with your hands? I often see people holding their hands in front of their body or behind their backs. Others put one hand in a pocket or on their hip. I have even seen someone fold their arms during a pitch. Do not do any of the above. Leave your hands by your sides and allow yourself to gesture as you would normally, as if you were chatting with someone. Of course, do not use gestures that block your face or become distracting to your audience. Do not use gestures that come across as aggressive, such as pointing your finger or using your fist. The right gestures, if they come naturally, can really reinforce your message.

Eyes

There is an old saying that 'the eyes are the windows to the soul'. Eye contact is incredibly important during a presentation. When presenting, I have seen many people look at the floor, the ceiling, the wall, out the window – anywhere but at the people they are talking to. What does this say to your audience? In Western culture it can often be disrespectful not to look people in the eye when you are talking to them. If you are talking to, but not looking at your audience, the perception may be that you do not care what the audience thinks.

People in Western culture look at you when you are speaking, and decide 'Do I like her?', 'Do I trust her?', 'Do I want to do business with her?' If you are not looking at the audience, they do not have that opportunity to make up their mind about you. It has already been made up. It will be 'no'.

I am not suggesting that you glare at people, or make anyone feel uncomfortable. However, it is important to look at people on the left, the right and in the middle of the room. A mistake that people often make is to concentrate on one side of the room; I have noticed, in speakers, that the direction their toes are pointed often dictates the direction they focus their energy. In doing so, you exclude the rest of your audience, though they are all watching you. If you are not looking at them and addressing them, they will get fed up, begin fidgeting or looking at their phones, and their minds will wander. They will begin to think, 'What time will this be finished?' or 'What will I wear out this evening?'

As I mentioned earlier, when one part of the audience starts to lose interest, it can have a ripple effect on the rest of the room. You want to be inclusive, not exclusive. Do not be afraid to look people in the eye.

I understand that some people are nervous and do not like

looking at people when speaking in public. They would prefer to look anywhere but at the audience. This can also come across as lacking confidence, or being unsure of your subject matter. I have even seen some people looking over the heads of their audience, but you really need to connect with your audience, and this is done by making eye contact. If you want to be believed, have an impact and get your message across, if you want investment or, indeed, any response from the audience – look them in the eye when you are speaking to them. Be aware that, in other countries, such as Japan, looking someone in the eye can be taken as a sign of disrespect. Obviously, in inter-cultural communication, it is important to respect the other person's culture.

Another reason for eye contact is that you need to be able to read your audience, and you cannot do this if you are looking out the window. You need to look at your audience and ask yourself 'Are they following my train of thought?' or 'Are they lost and confused?' To answer these questions, you need to read the body language of your audience. If you see lines appearing on their foreheads, or confused looks on their faces, you need to pause, and either give a recap or ask if everything makes sense, or whether there are any questions.

If you are addressing a particularly large audience then you are not going to be able to look directly at everyone in the room, however, if the audience is comprised of only four or five people, you should be able to connect with each one of them.

If one person asks you a question, you do not need to look at them the entire time you give a potentially lengthy answer. My suggestion would be, in giving your answer, to look at the person who asked the question sixty percent of the time, and look at the rest of the audience for the remaining forty percent of the time.

Are the eyes the windows to the soul? I do not know. I do

know that now, more than ever, we need to look an individual or a group of people in the eye when we are speaking with them. With so many people using smartphones, we are losing the habit of regular eye contact – it sometimes feels as if we cannot have a face-to-face conversation anymore without checking our phones.

Of all of the body language techniques worth remembering, eye contact is probably the easiest and the most important. If you have something important to say, do not look at the floor or the ceiling, or at the wall or out the window. If you look the person in the eye when you are speaking to them, it will lead to a belief that you know what you are talking about, that you can be trusted, that you care about them and that you mean business. Bare your soul.

Craft your delivery

As you can see, it is not enough to just speak. It is up to you to engage your audience, and you need to put some thought into the delivery of your message. You cannot expect your audience to listen simply because you are speaking. You need to command the room and the message. Crafting your content is very important, but crafting the delivery is equally important, if not more so.

What is the point of having the best content in the world if people cannot hear you? It would be a shame for them to become distracted from your message because of your delivery.

Focus on practising your delivery. Practise in front of a mirror, and record yourself so that you can listen for the variety within the voice. If it is not there, work on it. A great way to practise is by reading children's stories out loud. Take *Goldilocks and the Three Bears*, for instance. Each character has a different pitch within their voice; make it sound interesting. If you do not sound interesting how do you expect anyone in the audience to be interested? Your passion and enthusiasm need to come through in your voice. If they do, it will have a ripple effect on your audience. If you come across as lethargic and boring, it will also have a ripple effect. Which ripple do you want to create?

Managing nerves

In an *Irish Times* article, 'Treating a Performance of Stage Fright', 9 October 2012, Dr Muiris Houston said that:

> Performance anxiety or stage fright is classified by psychiatrists as a particular form of social anxiety disorder (also known as social phobia). Social phobia affects about eight percent of the population and is characterised by blushing, excessive sweating and stammering, all of which are triggered by a persistent fear of being judged harshly when in others' company. Those with social phobia are intensely self-critical of themselves while in company and experience a fear of being judged harshly by others.

From my experience in pitch coaching, a great deal more than eight percent of the population have 'performance anxiety'. Nerves are both normal and good. Any decent actor will tell you that they are nervous before a stage performance, and if you did not have nerves, your performance would be boring. You simply need to know how to manage your nerves, and find out what works for you.

Why are you nervous? Is it because it feels like a spotlight is on you? Then it is up to you to change that spotlight to a floodlight, and deflect it back onto your audience. It is not about you – it is entirely about the audience, and what you want the audience to do, think or feel as a result of what you are saying.

Are you nervous because you do not know your topic? Then keep practising until you know it inside out. Practise saying it in different ways, though, and do not learn it off by heart. Use keywords to help you to follow your train of thought.

Are you afraid you will go blank? Well, think of it this way: have you ever gone blank when telling a story to a group of friends? I doubt it. Think of your presentation like a story that you are telling to friends over coffee. You can tell the same story lots of different ways, but the message will still be the same. I have often found that people have a greater chance of going blank when they have learned something off by heart. Do not put unnecessary pressure on yourself to learn your story off by heart – just get better at telling your story.

Think of a swan: calm on the surface of the water, and paddling frantically underneath. You need to appear calm, regardless of how fast your heart may be beating. Find a way that works for you. Delivering a pitch, presentation or speech is like a stage performance. The late Irish actress Maureen Potter admitted that she suffered from 'performance anxiety', and was routinely physically sick before performances. She is known to have said that, on the occasions she was not actually sick, her performance was not as polished. I am not suggesting that you get physically sick before you deliver a speech, but I do suggest that you find a technique that works for you. Combine any of your preferred techniques with preparation and practice, and you should be quietly confident that all will go well.

Visualise yourself: you look good as you walk to the podium, standing tall. Place your notes on the lectern, check that the microphone is on, take a deep breath, smile and address your audience slowly and clearly, using eye contact.

Find a technique that works for you to manage nerves. I have some suggested techniques here.

Mindful-breathing meditation

This is my favourite technique for calming any nerves: just focusing on your breath, and nothing else. You can do this in a seat in a crowded room before going up to a podium to speak. It helps to ground you, and takes you out of the past and the future. All that matters, then, is the present moment. It can be done for five minutes or one minute – even thirty seconds of mindful-breathing meditation does the trick for me. It pauses the negative chatter that goes on in your head when you are nervous. Pause for however long it takes, and your mind will be much clearer when you return to your thoughts.

Positive affirmations

Instead of letting negative thoughts creep into your mind before a presentation, consciously choose your thoughts. Pick out a couple of short, positive sentences and repeat them in your mind. 'I deliver an excellent presentation. The audience love my speech. I get the investment I am looking for.' Keep repeating your positive sentences (out loud, if possible) until you start to believe them. This could be done in the car on the way to your event. Switch off the radio and continue saying your positive affirmations out loud until you arrive.

Visualisation

In November 2007 I interviewed award-winning British actor Giles Terera for a radio piece that I was doing in college called 'Fear of Public Speaking'. At the time, Terera was playing the lead role in J. M. Synge's *The Playboy of the Western World*, in the Abbey Theatre. It was an adaptation made by Roddy Doyle, one of Ireland's best loved writers, and Bisi Adigun, the founder of Arambe Productions, Ireland's first African Theatre Company.

I managed to get a ticket to the sold-out event the night

before the interview. It was a wonderful production, and I had never seen anything like the energy that Giles had on stage. The following day I interviewed him in the empty auditorium of the Abbey Theatre. He spoke about his terrible fear of public speaking and a visualisation technique he had developed to overcome it.

> It's the first entrance on stage that is the scary part. Adrenalin and nerves are always present at the start of any performance. I found that my first scene on stage was often spoiled by my nerves, but then once that scene was out of the way, I would calm down and wish that I could start all over again. I developed the visualisation technique to trick myself into feeling that I had already been out on stage in front of a great, responsive house, so that when I made my first entrance, it didn't feel like my first entrance and I could hit the ground running.

Giles would go out on stage about an hour before every performance and visualise a full house. He would imagine everyone sitting in their seats, and people standing at the back, in the aisles and at the sides. He would visualise telling a joke. He would visualise telling the joke step by step until he reached the punchline, when everyone would burst into laughter. He would breathe in the energy that he got from that visualisation technique, and then go into the dressing room to put on his costume. He would be back on stage less than an hour later, bursting with energy and confidence. Giles would do this every single night before a performance, and it worked. He still uses it, eight years on.

Relaxation technique

There are a couple of relaxation techniques you can try without anyone even knowing, while sitting in your seat. The first is to tense and relax your muscles from your toes right up to your forehead. Another technique is to place your hands under your seat and try to lift the seat from under you, which tenses all the muscles from your hands up to your shoulders and neck. When you let go of the seat, your upper body will feel relaxed.

Exercise

For some people, a brisk walk in the park, a jog, going to the gym or even a having a cycle can help with nerves the morning of a pitch or presentation. Try using up some of that extra nervous energy.

Practise

Keep going over and over your pitch as many times as possible, in front of the mirror, a video camera or even your cat – anyone who will listen. There is no substitute for practice.

Just do it

As the Facebook slogan says, 'Done is better than perfect'. Do your best. When you are finished, pat yourself on the back, and say 'Well done' to yourself for doing it. Then do a post-presentation analysis, learn from your mistakes and do it even better the next time.

Graphic harvesting done by Naomi Fein, founder of Think Visual.

Chapter Ten

CORPORATE PRESENTATIONS

How do corporate presentations differ from pitches? In essence, they do not. The objective is still the same: to get the message across clearly and concisely to the audience. Corporate presentations often go on for far too long, with too many slides filled with text and graphs that people cannot read. The audience are often bored, and the message gets lost.

Audience

As with any form of public speaking, the starting point of corporate presentations is always the audience. Who are they? What do they need to hear? Why should they care? What do they know about the topic already? How can you connect with them? What do you want them to do, think or feel by the time they leave the room?

The American author Maya Angelou once said, 'I've learned that people will forget what you said, people will forget what you did, but people will never forget how you made them feel.'

Content

The content of the presentation should be tailored to that particular audience. You might be asked to deliver the same presentation to different departments within the organisation, and the presentation should be tailored to each particular department. Of course, the majority of the content is the same, but examples, anecdotes or case studies should be relevant to each department. What is the story? What message needs to be delivered? Start with the story. Only when you have the story clear in your head should you then start thinking about slides.

Delivery

Ultimately, it is all about the delivery of the message, from your posture, gestures, eye contact, movements, and facial expression, to the variation of pitch and pace in your voice. Use pauses, and add emphasis. Speak loudly and clearly, pronouncing all of the vowels and consonants.

Managing slides

When asked to deliver a corporate presentation, some people think it is all about a set of slides, and that the presentation begins and ends with slides. This is not so. You should pare back the number of slides and the amount of text on those slides. If you have been asked to deliver a presentation, it is because of your knowledge and expertise. If they had wanted to just read off slides, you would have been asked to e-mail the PowerPoint presentation rather than taking up people's time at a meeting. The slides are there to support your message, but you need to deliver that message. The slides are not the presentation – you are.

When using slides, do not block the audience's view by standing in front of the display, and do not turn around to look back at the slides. Position your iPad or laptop in front of you so you can quickly glance at the screen and talk to the audience. Make sure the text is large enough to see at a glance. Use images where possible. Avoid full sentences, and use bullet points.

If used as a prompt, slides can help you get your message across. However, they can become a hindrance if not used properly, and can even take away from your message.

Use:

- Images instead of words;

- Keywords, not full sentences;

- Fonts large enough for people to see, especially in graphs and tables;

- Colours that people can read clearly.

Avoid:

- Standing in front of the slide;

- Looking back at the slide;

- Reading from the slide;

- Putting your whole presentation on to slides.

Answering questions

It is a positive sign when people ask questions after a presentation; it means that they are interested in what you have spoken about. I would suggest stating, at the outset, whether you want to wait and handle questions at the end of the presentation, or whether you are happy to be interrupted during your talk. I recommend leaving the questions to the end, as you may end up covering the answers later on in your presentation, and run the risk of repeating yourself. You also risk getting caught up in a discussion that brings you off topic. You may not get back to finishing your presentation, or you may end up rushing through the last few slides so as to finish on time.

It is not about whether you know the answer to the question or not, but how you handle the question. There are many ways a question can be answered.

Do not go on the defensive – listen to what is being asked. If you know the answer, answer the question as concisely as possible. If you do not know the answer, say so. Do not bluff or waffle, just be honest and remember that it is not what you say, but how you say it.

You could say, adding emphasis: 'That's a very *interesting* question. To be *honest*, I have never been *asked* this before.' Or, 'I have never *thought* about that before. I do not *know* the answer, but I will *find out* for you and I will get back to you on it by *tomorrow*, if that is okay.'

You could put the question to one of your colleagues, if they are with you in the room, or ask a specific person in the audience if you think they might know the answer: 'Peter, you worked on this before, is it something you could share with us?' You could also ask the question to the audience as a whole: 'Has anyone here come across this before?'

If you feel that the answer is not relevant to the audience as a whole, you might like to suggest a one-to-one meeting at a later time with the person who asked the question.

Your voice, body language and choice of words when answering questions are as important as during the presentation itself.

Interview with Joseph G. Lannig, Sales Director with Disney-ABC Television Group

I develop new sales relationships as well as managing existing ones. My number-one objective is to generate advertising sales for the ABC-owned television stations. I have been in this role for twenty-five years. This group provides 24/7 live local television to the following US television markets: New York, Los Angeles, Philadelphia, Houston, San Francisco, Fresno, Raleigh-Durham and Chicago. My division's goals are to generate sales revenue.

My presentations/pitches are designed to entice advertisers to commit their advertising dollars to our local television markets. My goal is to provide persuasive reasons as to why we are the best choice for their advertising needs.

In regards to preparation, I uncover pertinent background information on the company I am presenting to. My goal is to uncover the company's needs and objectives. I tailor my presentations to fulfilling their needs, and growing their business.

I practise my pitch beforehand. I usually create a written draft or notes, which I formulate into my final presentation. As television is the ultimate visual medium, I use live examples of our programming to lure and secure interest from our potential clients. PowerPoint is the base that I use to create my presentations.

I sometimes use notes. It varies depending on the topic, the length of the presentation and the time allotted. In longer presentations I like to highlight key terms or sections of my pitches to keep me on-message.

I try to keep most of my pitches under twenty-minutes long. My goal is to entice and stimulate the group, and I find that potential clients are thankful when they receive concise and shorter presentations.

I started selling thirty-two years ago, and I was fortunate to start in the sales training programme for the Xerox corporation. In 1983, Xerox and IBM where considered two of the top sales training programmes. We prepared with extensive role playing and presentations. As I have found throughout my professional sales career, there is no substitute for practise.

My presentations are more concise than when I started in 1983; I have learnt the importance of capturing the audience in the first minute or two. People want to be mildly entertained. It is the job of the presenter to quickly gain their interest.

A key concept that I use to prepare my presentations with is 'SPIN'. SPIN is an acronym for situation, problem, implications and needs. All of my successful presentations have been formulated in this fashion. One must fully understand the situation that the client is currently experiencing in the marketplace. 'Problems' comprises of what competitive or market forces are being encountered by their company that I may be able assist with. 'Implications' concerns whether I am able to provide a possible solution, and what impact or implications this solution will have on their company. Increased sales or productivity, for example. And lastly, needs. If I can provide this solution that we have agreed is helpful, will this solve your current situation and help your office morale and possibly your bottom line?

Storytelling is probably one of society's greatest traditions. People want to be entertained and stimulated, and it is the presenter's job to fulfil those desires and entice the audience. The story must be both concise and entertaining.

Successful pitching or presenting always comes down to practice, practice and more practice. You are the expert on your business or topic, but always be humble and empathic in your delivery. You need to entertain and win your audience over in the first minute or two.

There are only a few people in life that really influence you. In my studies at Boston College I encountered Professor Charles Lawson. He was in his eighties, and handicapped with severe arthritis in the hands. He was a professor who loved to extol the virtues of public speaking. No matter what pain he was in, his goal was to entice and stimulate his students. My mother, who was a grade-school teacher, always emphasised how sincerity, clarity, practice and a smile will go a long way. I am forever indebted to those two individuals for their insights.

Interview with Orla Gallagher, HR Specialist and Executive Coach at ESB

What mistakes do you see in corporate presentations?

The mistakes I see in corporate presentations are having too much detail in slides, and too many slides ('death by PowerPoint'). Presentations can sometimes also be too technical, especially in a technical company. Presenters forget to talk to their audience. Poor public speaking competence, a lack of preparation or presentations that are too long are also mistakes that presenters often make.

What, in your opinion, are the elements of an effective corporate presentation?

- Preparation and a deep understanding of your audience. Each presentation should be tailored to meet the requirements of the audience.

- Presenters need to really know their topic and speak with confidence – slides are a guide, not a crutch. Tell your story, talk to the audience and engage them. It is important to understand that the audience will not learn or retain everything in one presentation.

- Take into account the different learning styles of your audience: auditory, visual and kinaesthetic. Prepare your slides and presentation accordingly.

- If you need to give a detailed technical presentation, have two slide packs prepared, one for presenting, in which you follow the rules of PowerPoint and use visuals, correct colours and have very little information on each slide, and a second slide pack as a hand-out following the presentation, giving more detailed information.

Interview with Brian Bowden, Director of HR Operations, Aer Lingus

No matter how much an individual employee knows on a given topic, it is usually their ability to share this knowledge that really delivers value for the organisation. I think it is also important to take a broad perspective on what we mean by effective presentations: it means far more that the formal fifteen-minute PowerPoint. Each conversation an employee has with a colleague is an opportunity to present effectively; each interaction a frontline employee has with a guest is an opportunity to effectively present Aer Lingus.

Two common mistakes encountered in presentations are:

- Presenters giving too much data, and not enough analysis of what the data means;

- Presenters not considering their topic from the audience's point of view, and therefore not landing their message appropriately.

An effective corporate presentation has:

- An understanding of and focus on the needs of the audience;

- A structure that contextualises the issue, analyses the issue or data and summarises findings and recommendations;

- Delivery of information, not data.

Chapter Eleven

PRESENTING YOURSELF
FOR INTERVIEW

When presenting yourself for an interview, you are, effectively, pitching yourself. It might be an interview for a course, an award, a job or a promotion. Whatever the reason for your interview, you owe it to yourself to put your best foot forward.

Preparation Before the Interview

Know your application form

You cannot assume that the interviewer knows anything about you except what you have written in your application. Many interviewers will not have had a chance to look at your application in great detail. Just because you have mentioned something on the application form does not mean that the interviewer has picked up on it. Make a list of experience, further education, personal achievements and awards from your application that you do not want to leave the interview without mentioning, even if you have not been asked directly. They can be carved into your answers to other questions, included in an exchange at the end of your interview.

Guidelines, job specifications and person specifications

The organisation has drafted a set of guidelines for the position you are interviewing for. Examine them carefully. Underline the keywords that stand out for you. You need to try to match that list, so make sure that you tailor your answers and experience to the job specification and its requirements. It is unlikely that any candidate will be a one hundred percent match. You have been invited for interview, and they are interested in you and your experience. In the short space of time provided by an interview you will be unable to relate the complete detail of all of your experience, so pick and choose the golden nuggets of your experience that most match the outline they have set. At this point in your interview preparation, you need to remember that it is not about what you want to say but rather what the interviewer wants and needs to hear in order for you to secure the position.

Two possible questions

There are two questions often asked in an interview that you can definitely prepare for in advance. I would suggest, at most, a sixty-second answer to each.

One opening question might be: 'Can you tell me about your career to date?'

Another question could be: 'Can you tell me why you are the best person for this position?'

Even if neither question is asked in your interview, it is useful to prepare the answers to both, as it helps to sharpen your mind for the interview.

Other possible questions

Below are some potential questions to consider as part of your interview preparation. It would be worth your while making a list of additional questions you think could be asked during the interview, based on the application form or job specification.

- Tell me about yourself.

- What motivates you?

- What can you contribute to the team?

- How do you handle stress?

- What are your strengths?

- What are your weaknesses?

- How do you handle criticism?

- What interests you about this position?

- What particular experience do you have that you could bring to this position?

- What qualities do you think will be required for this position?

- What challenges are you looking for in a position?

- Where do you want to be in five years?

During the Interview

Competency-based interviews

Many interviews nowadays are based around competency. The interviewer will look for specific examples of how you have behaved in the past. Instead of you saying, 'This is what I can do or would do', you need to give examples of what you have done. This gives the interviewer a better indication of how you will behave in the future. If 'leadership' is one of the competencies listed in the job specification, for example, you might be asked, 'Can you tell me about a time when you showed exceptional leadership skills?'

It is important to have at least five case scenarios ready for the interview: short and snappy examples relating to keywords from the job specification. It might be 'problem-solving', 'decision-making', 'organisational skills' or 'time management'. Notice that I have said that the examples should be short and snappy – you do not want to bore the interviewer with long-winded stories. Relate the situation you were in at the time, the action you took and the positive result that followed.

Effective Communication

Everything discussed in Chapter Nine on delivery applies to an interview situation: shake hands, use people's names, make eye contact. Be conscious of your posture when entering the room and when sitting in your seat – your shoulders should be back and your feet should be flat on the floor. Have a pleasant facial expression. Speak loudly enough for people to hear you. Vary the pitch and the pace of your voice. Do not speak too quickly. Use pause and add emphasis. Sound interested.

Interview with Ken Cowley, Recruitment Consultant at Headhunt International

Wherever possible, the Headhunt International recruitment agency bring people into their offices to talk to them in person before recommending them to a potential employer. In addition to this, they may do another prep interview, or have a conversation on the phone with the potential candidate, to help to prepare them.

The meeting with the recruitment agency is effectively part one of the job interview, because the recruitment agency must put you forward for the job in the first place. Treat the meeting with the recruitment agency as you would a job interview.

It is important to dress smartly for the interview, whether meeting with the recruitment agency or the potential employer. This typically means a jacket, shirt and tie, or the female equivalent.

Some people say, 'Oh, it's much more informal these days, especially in the software industry,' but it is better to err on the side of caution. If it turns out that everyone is very casual, you can take off your jacket or remove your tie, but it is better to arrive prepared.

The day before your interview is quite important in terms of your preparation. You should be researching the job and the company and going over the job specification. When reading it in detail and checking the keywords that are used, think of ways of presenting yourself tailored to those words. For example, if they are looking for a 'self-starter' or a 'hunter' – an expression often used in sales positions – they want someone who will go out and actively seek and obtain business, not a passive person who will wait for the phone to ring. Use that job specification to make a list of points that you will refer to in the interview.

Whether your interview is via Skype or in person, have your CV with you. Bring a couple of copies just in case, and offer a copy to whoever is interviewing you. Know your CV well. Many people have different versions of their CV, so remember which version you sent. Know that CV, and be prepared to answer questions based upon it. If on your CV you have said that you are X, Y or Z, be prepared to back up each claim.

One of the early questions is likely to be along the lines of, 'What can you do for us?' or 'What are your biggest selling points?' There may be a few preamble questions, such as, 'What were your responsibilities in your recent jobs?' These are also important questions, but the first key question is, 'What can you do for us?' Be prepared to get straight in and wow them, showing how you are going to be indispensable to them and how you will tick all of their boxes, with what you believe they are looking for.

Be open to the interview going in a different direction to that which you prepared for. For example, if the interviewer says, 'We also want someone who can do this', be prepared to be flexible. Always appear willing and open to go the extra mile. Smile and be positive. A lot of people do not smile during interviews. You need to show that you want the job through your body language and tone of voice. These are both hugely important, especially if the job is a public-facing position. They will be taking note of how you engage with people. The interview should sell this aspect of your personality better than the cover letter will have done.

As recruitment agents, candidates often ask us who is going to be on the interview panel. We do a lot of recruitment for the medical profession, and the interview panel will quite often include a consultant, a clinical director and someone from human resources. We let the candidate know so that they can research the person involved, and check whether they have had any material published.

Competency-based interviews, focusing on examples of what candidates have done in the past that match the job specification, are still very popular. Questions may include: 'Give me an example of how you overcame an adverse situation in the past' or 'How did you overcome a poor sales period?' Have a good example ready, demonstrating how you handled the situation. For example, 'I went in and did this extra campaign', or 'We had a very big problem with a customer, so I went out and met with them and worked through the problem in this way.' Give a concrete example.

Listen to the question, and answer what is being asked. People tend to waffle, especially when they are nervous. You may have an answer ready, or you may need to speak off the cuff, but your answer should, at most, be no longer than one or two minutes. You may have only been allocated fifteen or twenty minutes for the interview.

At the end of the interview, you may be asked whether you have any questions. You could ask questions such as, 'What is the team that I would be working with like?' or 'What is the culture like in the office?' You could ask about the future plans for the company, or what opportunities exist for you there. Whatever you ask, show your interest, and how well you have researched the company. Even if you have not got any questions, there is no harm in reiterating your interest in the job, and why you feel you are the best person for the position. Often, a final question during an interview will be: 'Could you sum up why you are the perfect candidate for the role?'

A final checklist would be:

- Make a list of the likely questions you might get asked.

- Do a dry run.

- Get a good night's sleep.

- Do not eat anything unwise the night before, and avoid alcohol.

On the day itself, get up early, leaving yourself plenty of time. Know where you are going, and arrive at least twenty minutes early – but do not enter the building more than five minutes early. Do not drink too much coffee before your interview, as that can sometimes cause people to perspire or become fidgety. If the company offers you tea, coffee or water, we suggest taking water, unless everyone is having tea or coffee. Take a deep breath, relax and good luck.

Interview with Orla Gallagher, HR Specialist and Executive Coach at ESB

The interview is one part of the selection process. Human resources spend a considerable amount of time and expertise short-listing candidates prior to the interview itself.

We sometimes require candidates to deliver presentations during the interview for certain campaigns, either for internal or external positions – graduate engineers, for example. If required, the presentation would take ten to fifteen minutes, and happen at the beginning of the interview. The title of the presentation is dependant on the position, and would be relevant to it.

The type of interview (competency-based interview, that is) is the same for internal and external interviews, and they are both graded in the same way. The interview process changes according to the position and the part of the company that is recruiting.

All interview questions are based on competencies. Our interviewers are skilled, and specially trained in this type of interviewing.

In terms of preparation, I would suggest that candidates spend time reviewing their competencies, and thinking of clear examples of how they have demonstrated each competency. It takes a considerable amount of time to prepare for an interview.

As regards the interview panel, it generally comprises of someone from human resources, a technical expert and a line manager. There is normally a gender balance, with human resources chairing the interview.

All interview processes, including those at ESB, have standards that they expect candidates to adhere to. Impact and communication are very important throughout the interview, as is good interviewee ethic. Most importantly, the candidate must be able to effectively demonstrate that they have the required competencies and technical ability to do the advertised role.

Interview with Brian Bowden, Director of HR Operations at Aer Lingus

We often require candidates for senior specialist or management roles to deliver a presentation during the interview, on a current topic that is directly impacting the role they are applying for.

The interview process is the same in Aer Lingus for internal and external candidates, and both are graded the same.

There are always a number of generic questions used in interviews, for example, 'Discuss your previous relevant experience' or 'Why have you applied for the role?' These questions help the interviewer to understand the candidate's experience for the current role, and what their motivation for working within the company is.

I would suggest that the candidate review the vacancy notice in great depth. This includes reviewing the job description (what the job will entail) and the person specification (the requirements of the role) and researching the company. This will ensure that, prior to the interview, the candidate understands the role and the company (and the industry that the company operates in), and is aware of what is required to carry out the role.

The candidate should then examine their CV to identify similarities between the job and person descriptions, and their own experience and skills. In relation to the person specification, it is important that the candidate understand the requirements listed, and have prepared examples in which they demonstrate the skills that were required in their past roles. It is also important that the candidate has thought about what he or she can bring to the role, and what the role can do for them, from a developmental, progression or career perspective.

The interview panel generally consists of a line manager, a senior manager and human resources.

Often candidates:

- Do not spend ample time preparing fully for interviews, so they do not fully understand the job description and person specification.

- Do not fully listen to the question asked.

- Provide answers that lack focus and do not fully answer the question asked.

I would just emphasise that we are often:

- Presenting in informal settings without notice.

- Being interviewed outside of the interview situation.

These situations represent great opportunities to someone who tries to understand their audience, structure their thoughts and deliver value through insights and informed commentary.

Interview with Garrett Taylor, Fleet Captain at Aer Lingus

I am a line standards captain (LSC) on our Airbus A330 fleet. I conduct the interviews for three pilot positions within Aer Lingus, with the first being for cadet pilots. The candidates applying for this position are hoping to become trainee pilots with Aer Lingus, who would then partially sponsor their training in flight school, currently conducted in Jerez, Spain. On completion of their basic training, we bring them back to Dublin and place them on a course to become co-pilots on our European jet fleet. They generally remain with us for their entire flying career. It is a very sought-after position. The last intake was in 2015, and twelve cadets were chosen from 5,000 applicants.

The second position I conduct interviews for is direct-entry pilots. These candidates will already have a small amount of commercial flight experience, or have just finished flight school themselves. They will usually be employed on a full-time basis.

The third position I conduct interviews for is for contract pilots. These candidates have a certain amount of commercial flight experience, and will be employed on short-term contracts.

The recruitment process consists of an online application and psychometric testing, and an initial interview, attended by Aer Lingus and conducted for us by the flight-training school. The final interview is conducted by two operating captains, and a member of our human resources team. This is followed by a medical and a psychological assessment.

In addition to the technical requirements of each role, I look, more importantly, for a good set of interpersonal skills and a proven motivation.

Effective communication is very important, as information exchanged in the cockpit has to be clear, concise and accurate. We measure that, firstly, by whether the candidate listens to the question and secondly, if the candidate answers the question accurately and precisely. I do not mind periods of silence, as it can indicate the thought process that the candidate is engaging in to achieve the above goal. Interview candidates should not be afraid of these short periods of silence while optimising their answers.

Both tone and body language are important aspects of communication, as are timing, requesting feedback that your message has been received and understood and conflict resolution. A high standard of interpersonal skills is required, so eye contact, a good handshake and using your interviewer's name are all very important. We do measure these skills. All of these aspects are important, right from the start. Everybody is nervous, but a smile is a great way of putting people at ease.

Dressing appropriately for the interview is very important. We are not looking for fashion statements or designer clothes, but we expect shiny shoes, clean suits and well-ironed shirts. We like our pilots to look the part at all times.

The opening question is meant to relax the candidate. If they are relaxed then we get the best out of them, and can therefore get a better picture of the real person sitting in front of us. This is important – picking the wrong candidate is very costly. An opening question involves asking them to tell us about themselves, and what they have been doing for the last five years. They talk us through the answer and usually settle in to the interview.

Mistakes I often see are when candidates do not listen to the question, or giving long-winded answers. It is important to be able to honestly say that you do not know the answer to the question, if that is the case. Remember to never swear – I have heard it in interviews, and it never comes across as impressive.

My advice for candidates preparing for interviews is:

- Research the company you are applying to. Know their facts and figures, current operating levels and projected growth.

- Be able to describe yourself in as little as five words: hard-working, disciplined, self-motivated, and so on.

- Be able to describe the qualities required to work in the position you are applying for.

- Practise out loud and get used to the sound of your own voice delivering interview answers.

- Know as much as you can about the position you are applying for – work shifts, responsibilities, advantages and disadvantages (all of which you will be able to overcome).

- Put yourself in the shoes of the interviewer. They have probably conducted at least six detailed interviews that day, and must write a report on each candidate. There is nothing as satisfying as seeing someone with all the required skills, delivering the correct answers and sitting there confidently, enjoying themselves while entertaining you.

- It is a race. Be your best, be competitive and, most importantly, finish strong. You do not have to ask questions, but feel free to clarify anything that may have been unclear during the interview. Leave a lasting impression of yourself with the interview panel, and make sure that they remember your name.

Chapter Twelve

MEDIA INTERVIEWS

'How do you get a media interview about your start-up?' you may ask. 'How do you get interviewed by the *Irish Times* about your new business?' or 'How do you get an opportunity to speak on radio or appear on television, to tell everyone about how your new product will change the world?' If you have not dealt with the media before and you have a sizeable budget, there are plenty of public relations companies to guide you through the media experience.

Interview with Graeme Slattery, Managing Director of the PR Company Notorious PSG

We are first and foremost a public-relations agency, dealing with media relations and coverage generation, social-media strategy and community management, event-development and execution, experiential, brand strategy and development and much more.

A company uses a press release when they have news that they want to drive consumer awareness around. A press release serves as a one-stop informational piece that can deliver the news, provide relevance to the audience – the media and the public – and explain why they should sit up and take notice.

When delivering content in a press, radio or television interview, my advice would be to develop great stories, and tell them well. A good agency can help you with this. Make sure that you also get media training, so that when your time in the sun comes, you have the best chance to shine. Stick to the facts and be honest. Keep it brief, and use short sound bites to deliver your news rather than long, drawn-out sentences.

Know your audience, and speak to them on their level. The reporter is not your audience – the listeners or readers are.

The Press Release

If you are pitching yourself directly to the business editor of a newspaper, radio or television programme, one public relations technique is the press release. It can be a really effective way of getting your message across to the media. A successful press release simply consists of the right story, in the right place and at the right time. I work with Dublin City FM, and have two interview slots on the 'Good Morning Dublin' programme. I try to fill those slots with interesting content. I read press releases all the time looking for that content. It is quite often simply down to what interests me, but also about how engaging the content is, and whether I think my listeners would be interested also.

Interview with Simon Cocking, Editor of *Irish Tech News*

Here are his tips on writing a press release, published on Irish Tech News on 20 May 2015:

1. Answer the 'who, what, why, when, where, how' questions. We have had press releases that leave more questions unanswered than a mystery book.

2. What problem have you solved? Tell us, please. You launching a start-up or a product is not actually that interesting, unless you can tell me why you have done something interesting or useful to *me*, or someone I care about, somewhere in the world.

3. Do not include long, boring, quotes from politicians. If your product is good enough, then *you* tell us why.

4. Use simple language. Using jargon or acronyms just loses your audience's attention. It is actually smarter to be able to explain your product in plain English. If you cannot, then you have failed in your communication.

5. Less is more. Five hundred to seven hundred words is plenty.

6. Give us a headline. We may not use it, but at least you have given us an idea of what your three-second pitch is. Our attention spans are getting shorter and shorter.

7. Do not include capital letters in the title. It is shouting. You will get people's interest if your title and story are compelling enough.

8. Give us your social media details for accounts that you actually use and care about. People will read these articles about you, and some will even click on the links.

9. If you had not already guessed, humour is great. Don't sweat it. It is better to be clear, but if you can be funny, you might just make our day.

Interview with Pamela Newenham, *Irish Times* Business Journalist

Pamela Newenham works as a business journalist for the *Irish Times*. Pamela started off in the *Irish Times* as a news reporter in 2008, working in the courts, then on general news reporting. She has been working as a business journalist for the *Irish Times* for the last three and a half years.

According to Pamela, start-ups and entrepreneurs pitch to everyone. Sometimes the business editors get pitches, and sometimes the journalists get pitches. Sometimes another journalist will meet an entrepreneur who pitches to them, and the journalist will come back to the office and relate that pitch to a business journalist. Sometimes start-ups send a letter to another department, and then they will forward it on to the business department.

What is a pitch?

A pitch will depend on what the story is. If you are pitching for a news article, you should have a good press release that should outline what the news story is: if you are bringing out a new product, if you are moving to new offices or have bought new offices, if you are creating new jobs, or expanding into the United States. Anything that is news should be included in the press release.

There does not always have to be something new within your business to warrant contacting the business section of the *Irish Times*. You could send a pitch to a journalist for a feature or an interview.

Your pitch must be catchy. You must offer something different or unique. You need to think about what you can offer, and having a good backstory always helps. Offering exclusivity on this piece helps, too. In your pitch, you could write that you are only offering it to the *Irish Times* or whichever newspaper you are contacting. Give the journalist the first choice of declining or accepting.

I get around 400 emails a day. If I'm lucky, I'll get 300. If I was to respond to them all, I would get no work done.

Pitch content

In the subject line of the email you have to have a good word, like 'exclusive', and a line like 'Great story for . . . ' Then I'll open the email.

Do not write the subject line entirely in capital letters. Make sure that you get the journalist's name right. I get pitches that open with 'Hi Paula' or 'Hi Patricia' at least once a week, and then I do not really read any further. If they cannot even get my name right, why should I bother?

If it is for a feature or an interview, send a few paragraphs, but not a press release. You should have a catchy opening that you extend and develop. Then bring it back, but stick to four or five paragraphs. We do not have time to read twenty-five paragraphs.

I always carry out interviews either face-to-face or over the phone. For longer interviews, such as the 'Interview of the Week' published in the Friday edition of the *Irish Times*, I sit down with the interviewee in their workplace for at least one hour, and also get a tour to see and understand the whole business.

Mistakes in a press release

You will often see too much technical jargon in press releases. The person writing the press release is trying to use complicated phrases and words, when simple ones would do. They think it makes them sound better, but it does not. Sometimes there is too much nitty-gritty relating to operating systems or software. We have better things to do than trying to decipher complicated language.

Mistakes in an interview

Start-ups do not talk enough. The main mistake is they do not sell themselves the best they can, or that they do not come across as being as passionate as they should about their start-up. This is mostly due to shyness.

No preparation required

The entrepreneur does not have to prepare anything before the interview. If they know their business, they should be fine. They should talk more, and not give five-word answers to questions. It will just annoy the journalist, and leave them with a bad impression. If you do not know the answer, do not pretend that you know the answer. I cannot always tell when people are lying, but I once found out afterwards. I telephoned to question them, and they said that they had lied because they did not know the answer. I pulled the interview. I said, 'That is just not good enough. I could not trust you now.'

It is all about the content

When I am interviewing, it is all about the content. I am not concerned with body language or tone of voice. More often than not, I have my head down and am writing down everything they are saying. I do not record the interview and I never bring any questions. I ask another question based on what they have just said.

I always open with questions like, 'Tell me how your start-up came about,' or 'What was your light-bulb moment?' Sometimes, if it's dull, I throw in a few questions like, 'Tell me about something embarrassing that happened at work or in your career,' or 'What was the most challenging moment you had?' or 'What are the funny things that have happened in the business?'

That brings in the human element. You often get hilarious answers. I do not always publish an article after an interview – maybe ninety-six percent of the time. Sometimes the interviews are awful.

Pamela's tips for start-ups

- Talk more.

- Do not give five-word answers.

- Do not lie.

- Do not make the journalist's life difficult.

- Do not harass the journalist about when the interview will be published.

Interview with Victoria Mary Clarke, Author, Broadcaster, Journalist and Media Coach

Victoria noticed, over her twenty-five years as a print and broadcast journalist, that some people become very scared before media interviews. They are afraid of what they will sound like and what people will think of them, but they are also afraid of not saying the right thing. She set up her media-coaching business to try to help anyone who felt they needed some help with media interviews.

Radio interviews

A radio interview is meant to be a conversation. It is not an interrogation, and it is not an exam. When people come to me before a radio interview, I try to have a chat with them to get to know them a little bit, and then find out why they want to be on the radio, and what they want to say. If you do that, you can get to what they are actually about, and they usually have something they want to share. They might be a musician, a chef or a yoga teacher, but they always have something that they want to share, something that they are passionate about and that they are good at, and that is what you want to get to. When they get talking about their passion, they forget the 'How do I sound?' and 'What do I look like?' questions, and they actually just tell you the stuff you want to hear. That is what allows them to feel safe, what helps them feel enthusiastic. From a journalist's point of view, there is nothing as contagious or as uplifting as enthusiasm. Some people are afraid that we, the journalists, are bitches – that we are going to be mean to them, that there is a 'Simon Cowell' aspect to us and that we want to put them down and make them feel bad. But, generally, and thinking of the people I have met in the business, most of us are pretty nice.

I have heard that quite a few media coaches try to change the way people speak. Perhaps they are using words they shouldn't, or pausing or hesitating. I find that people then focus on the fault, and they are obsessed with their mistakes – 'How many times did I say "like"?' – or whatever it was. Then they forget about what they are there to say. You just have to talk about the thing that excites you. If it excites you, it excites us.

The journalist does not know what you want to say. They will talk to you until they have something they can use, but it is important to try to bring the conversation back to your thing – you may have a special offer at your restaurant, or a new restaurant, or a new training course that you really want people to know about. Do not feel intimidated by the interviewer. If he or she is leading you down a path that you do not want to go down, just say, 'You know what, I would love to talk about this . . . ' or 'That's a great question, but I would love to talk about this . . . '

If there is something in particular that you want to say, get it in early and get it in again before the interview wraps up. Have a friend interview you beforehand. Get them to ask you the questions, and even give them the questions to ask you, so that they are leading you down the path you want to go on. I would not recommend sending in pointers that you want to cover. I think that they can sometimes put people off. I know that I have been put off by people saying, 'This is what I want to talk about.' You might give them a bio or send them some material but, generally, journalists like to do their own research. They do not want to feel like you are pushing them in a particular direction.

Television interviews

In television people focus more on what they look like, what they are wearing, how their hair looks and whether they look fat. They focus on that kind of thing, more than on how they sound. In my experience, I have never noticed myself looking any different on television. People tend to be more self-conscious about how they look, and that can take over from the message. Put that out of your mind, and just remind yourself, when you are looking at people on television, you do initially focus on what they look like, but then when they start talking you become engaged with what they are saying, so it is important to have something to say.

As regards what to wear for a television interview, avoid stripes, as they can look quite blurry. I'm also not sure about black for television. I think Miriam O'Callaghan is a great person to emulate if you are a woman – she always looks amazing. She tends to wear block colours, and quite bright colours, like blues and greens and reds. Everybody has a phone with a camera now, and there is no excuse for not practising – get a friend to film you so you can see what you look like.

Concentrate on getting across what you are there to get across. You can still have a bit of fun with being on television. I have noticed that a lot of people look as though they are being interrogated when they are on television. It is not an interrogation, and you do not have to pretend that the cameras are not there. You do not have to pretend that you are not on television. You can acknowledge that you are in a studio with an audience.

Nerves

The first time I went on 'The Late Late Show', Pat Kenny was the host. I was scared, as it was my first time on live television. I had done other kinds of television – documentaries and that sort of thing – but never with an actual studio audience. A friend who practises reiki did reiki on me before the show. He stood around as I was going into the studio, and pushed a bit of extra reiki in as I stepped through the curtain – I just felt as though it was my sitting room and these were my friends, and like I had invited Pat Kenny to my house. I just felt completely at home. Even now, when I rewatch it, I think, 'How was I so relaxed?' Reiki is amazing for relaxation, as are yoga and deep breathing. Try to spend five or ten minutes doing some breathing exercises or mindful meditation. I have trained in reiki and yoga, so I am also a yoga teacher and a reiki practitioner. I use those techniques on my clients if they want.

I also recommend deep breathing. Once your breathing has changed, you slow down, and the main problem people have is speaking too fast.

Print journalism

As regards print, you are not being seen and you are not being heard, so it is more about the content, and more about giving a good story.

Chapter Thirteen

PUBLIC SPEAKING

Oratory, or public speaking, as it is now known, dates back thousands of years – well before an investment pitch or a corporate presentation. Speeches can have a powerful impact on people's hearts and minds.

One of Ireland's most famous speeches is that given by Pádraig Pearse, in August 1915, at the funeral of Jeremiah O'Donovan Rossa. There is a re-enactment of this speech at 2:30 PM at the grave of O'Donovan Rossa every day in Dublin's Glasnevin Cemetery. According to Annie Birney, education officer at the Glasnevin Cemetery Museum, Pearse was speaking not only about the life of O'Donovan Rossa and his belief in the cause of independence for Ireland, but was also encouraging those listening at the graveside to renew their vows of achieving that independence.

The speech that Pearse gave would make its mark on Irish history. O'Donovan Rossa's funeral is sometimes referred to as a 'dress rehearsal for the Easter Rising', which occurred the following year.

For the centenary of the 1916 Easter Rising, Annie Birney and Bridget Sheerin, both of whom work in the Education Department at Glasnevin Cemetery Museum, are running a workshop for schools in speech writing and delivery. The workshop draws its inspiration from the power of Pearse's words, and the speech which he is believed to have spent weeks preparing. In this workshop, students write speeches about the people buried in Glasnevin who had a positive impact on society during their lifetimes, through politics, art, literature, music or engineering.

In their speeches, Annie and Bridget encourage students to develop a clear introduction, a main body and a closing. Though not much is known about the exact manner in which Pearse delivered his speech, Annie and Bridget suggest these rules for speech delivery:

- Stand up straight.
- Make eye contact with the crowd.
- Use your facial expressions.
- Use gestures.
- Take a deep breath before speaking, and speak loudly and clearly.
- Speak slowly, and pronounce all your words.
- Avoid slang.

The same rules apply today as in 1915.

If you can try to master public speaking instead of avoiding it, you may actually enjoy it. For the audience to enjoy hearing your talk or speech, you need to enjoy delivering it.

If you have been asked to speak at an event – accepting an award for your business, for example – there is a certain amount of preparation required to ensure a positive outcome.

Speech Preparation

Find out as much information as possible about the event.

- What is the topic of your talk or speech?
- What is the duration of your talk or speech?
- Are you the main speaker?
- Who is speaking before you or after you?
- What have they been asked to speak about?
- Where will you deliver the speech?
- How many will be in the audience?
- Who will be in the audience?

Start thinking of random ideas you can bring into the content from the moment you are asked to deliver a talk or speech. Keep a notebook close by, to jot down ideas. It can often be late at night or first thing in the morning that you think of something. You could even be in the shower, or going for a walk in the park when you have that light-bulb moment.

You need to connect with your audience regardless of what you have been asked to speak about. That will determine the success of your talk or speech. You need to be very clear about what you want them to do, think or feel as a result of what you will say. By researching your audience and being clear about the message you want them to take away, you are well on your way to constructing your speech.

If you find it useful, use the two-minute mindful breathing meditation and creative brainstorming in Chapter Eight to brainstorm the content of your talk or speech. When you have done that, compare your notes with the ideas you have written in your notebook in the weeks beforehand. Look at all the notes together, and highlight the ones that stand out. More than likely, you are not going to be able to use everything in your notes. Use what you believe is most relevant to the topic and audience.

Crafting Your Talk or Speech

A well-crafted talk or speech will hold the attention of your audience. A rambling, poorly prepared speech will soon have their minds wandering.

The recipe, I believe, is very simple. I also mentioned it in Chapter Eight. It should include a wow opening, three points that follow a logical structure, and a closing that overlaps with the opening. Include a brief summary, a thank you and an action for the future. Imagine taking the audience by the hand, step-by-step through your talk. You want them hanging on to every single word. Leave the audience wanting more, as opposed to wanting you to wrap it up and sit down as quickly as possible.

Avoid long sentences

Using long sentences without any pauses can prove very difficult for your audience to take in. You may also lose your own train of thought halfway through a long sentence. It is better to use short, snappy sentences. They are easier for you to deliver, and easier for your audience to understand. Try to ensure that each point you make has a logical flow to the next one. If your points are in a random order it makes it much more difficult for the audience to follow, and they will give up trying.

Be inclusive

Be as inclusive as possible. Make sure that you pronounce people's names correctly, and avoid embarrassing or insulting anyone with any stories or anecdotes you include in your speech. The atmosphere can turn sour very quickly. Try to use the word 'you'; it is the most used word in marketing. It makes people feel as if you are speaking directly to them. Try and build that emotional connection between you and the audience. What do you and the audience have in common that you could bring into the speech? If you do not do any of these things, the audience may not like you.

Be heard

If people cannot hear you, there is no point in speaking. It is as simple as that. There is nothing more frustrating for the audience than straining to hear the speaker. It is your job, as a speaker, to check the acoustics in the room. If you need a microphone, get one. If you have a choice, a roaming mic is better than a fixed mic as it allows freedom of movement on the stage or away from the podium.

If it is a fixed mic, make sure that it is in the correct position and at the right height for you. Even with a microphone, make sure your voice projects. Speak slowly and clearly. Pronounce your vowels and consonants. Pause for effect and emphasise the keywords.

Be understood

Do not use technical jargon that the audience cannot understand.

Do not complicate your speech to make yourself appear intelligent. Keep your speech simple and understandable.

Be engaging

Do not just expect the audience to be interested. It is up to you to make the content of your talk as interesting and engaging as possible. You may be talking about a serious topic, but it does not have to be boring. Do your research, build up your facts, add your quotes, examples, case studies and anecdotes. Craft a logical structure to your message, and you will be well on your way to making your speech or talk interesting to your audience.

Be relevant

It is important to be relevant to your audience and with regard to the topic you have been asked to speak about. Do not go off-topic. I encourage creativity and using your imagination in your speech, but unless you can make it relevant to what you have been asked to talk about, leave it out. Listen to the speeches before you, and, if appropriate, do not be afraid to include a previous speaker in the content of your speech. It is a courteous way of showing that you have been listening to others in the room.

Be concise

Do not overload people with too much information – they will not remember everything you say, anyway. Cognitive psychologists tell us that people tend to remember things in threes, so craft your speech into three key messages. Write a sound bite for each message, and build a paragraph around each sound bite. Whatever you do, do not go over the time allocated to the speech, as it can knock the event totally out of sync.

Interview with Lawrence Bernstein, Managing Director of Great Speech Writing

When and why

I set up my company Great Speech Writing in 2005. I was working as a consultant for a number of firms in the city. My life was dominated by travel, writing presentations and delivering them, and the more insight I gained into the corporate world, the more I began to understand just how low the benchmark was for communication and presentations. I was often given material that was clearly not suited to the spoken word. There was a complete and utter disparity between the quality of work going on within an organisation, and the way that it was communicated.

My business started by mistake. A friend asked me to write his best-man's speech, which I dictated to him over a couple of beers. He suggested I do that sort of thing professionally, and I put an advertisement in *Private Eye* magazine, and got one speech from it. The business grew over the next couple of years from being a hobby, until I eventually gave up my day job.

I was finally able to have a more direct say in content. It was immediately clear that, with better content, speakers had much more confidence when it came to delivery.

Team and clients

I now have a team of five speech writers, and two people who manage the business itself. I have worked with a wide range of clients on their speeches – from CEOs in retail to heads of HR, medical people, a head of state, MPs in Australia, the European Parliament and the UK – as well as local politicians and councillors.

On the 'social' side, we have wedding speeches – when you get to hear the most interesting stuff, when you get to hear about people's lives. That is what makes this such a fun way to earn a living; you get to meet lovely people, and talk about some fun stuff as well. While everyone has a story to tell, they quite often do not realise, a) how good the stories are, and b) how to make the most of them.

Challenging speeches

Some of the toughest speeches to make, for clients, are for fundraising. It is difficult talking to big rooms full of people quite weary of the 'ask', and having to inspire and motivate and sell a cause to make money.

What the key is

The key to writing a really great speech is not being an expert in the subject.

There are three things that make a speech great. They are the basis upon which we built the business.

The first is relevance. It is very hard to be relevant unless you start by thinking about your audience, rather than thinking about yourself and the things you feel you have to talk about. The vast majority of poor speeches fall into the trap of focusing on the technical, on themselves and on the internals, and forgetting that the audience needs them translated into something relevant and appropriate to them.

What is it that is going to make the people in the room at that time open their eyes and really want to know more? It helps more to think from the perspective of an audience member.

The first questions I ask are 'What is the point?' and 'What do you want your audience to think when you sit down?'

Who is in the audience inside and outside the room? Who will read about it in the press? Who will click the link to watch it on video? Who will find it online?

Then we look at what is going to turn those people on. What is going to interest them? What is going to surprise them? What is going to make them do something that they have never done before? And what do you want that thing to be?

Relevance is the absolute guiding light to everything we do. It is number one.

Number two is clarity. It is very hard to deliver a great speech or pitch if you are rambling, or if you have got too many words. Some of our clients ask us to write material from scratch, and others ask us to take a look at what they have written. There are very few speeches we get, including those written professionally, where we cannot instantly scrap thirty percent of the words without losing any meaning at all. If you combine a really clear, easy-to-understand speech with something that is relevant, you are getting there.

Finally, the hard part: sprinkling magic onto it, somehow, to make it original, different and exciting. That one is hard to quantify, but that bit of magic is what sets it apart.

No formula, just a process

The formula is not to have a template, but a process.

We always start with a blank piece of paper. I could not tell you how that speech will work, but the process will always be the same. You gather information, and discuss relevance and agree on an approach. You then take the blank piece of paper, put all of the details to one side for a moment and write a series of very simple sub-headings. On their own, they should create a clear argument or plot that takes you from the beginning to the end. So you leave out all of the detail and all of the evidence, and just make a big-picture flow. That flow will be framed around the audience, topic and outcome. Then, generally, we use a split screen. On one side we have your beautiful, clean, sub-headed document, and on the other side you have all the notes you have taken, and all the ideas you have got.

If you read through those ideas and notes, you will begin to detect relevance in them. The biggest problem is dumping everything you have into a formula.

If you have a very clear argument, using a theme, using a touch of magic, you can pick and choose the bits that will work, and put them into the appropriate bit of the speech map. At that stage, it is not like a written document – it is more like a jigsaw, but a jigsaw where you only use thirty or forty percent of the pieces.

If you have a charity speech, for Syrian refugees, for example, there is the temptation to talk about everything – disease, overcrowding, hunger, children, cold. In the end, it becomes a bit of a blur. It is about picking and prioritising, and you can only do that if you have got an argument that you want to sustain.

Get the argument in place before you use the evidence. You will then be able to pick from that second screen, and just drop it all in. At this stage, you are not writing and you are not thinking about the beauty of the language. You end up with what looks like a random collection of notes, tied together by sub-headings.

That is when you stop reading and you stop researching. You have hit the point at which you cease to become a researcher, and then become a writer. From there, it is about writing beautifully.

Sub-headings

There is no limit to the sub-headings. The audience will never hear them – that is between the speech-writer and the speaker. It might be that over a ten-minute speech, you have seven, eight or nine sub-headings, and you spend a minute on each. The key, then, is linking each one. It is all in the writing, and how seamlessly you can make the links.

If you get the hook wrong at the start, that is where you begin to lose your audience. The end also matters, but there is a real danger that speech-writers spend fifty percent of their time on the opening, closing and the sound bites, and then dump the evidence in the middle. You need to exude relevance and quality right from the beginning, and then all the way through.

Story

The story element depends on the subject. You could have a speech that is a story. You could have a speech that absolutely avoids them. It is very hard to generalise. There is a danger that long stories with punchlines can rely entirely on the quality of delivery. A stand-up comedian can get away with it, but a lot of senior people in business and politics cannot. I am much more of a believer in dropping in short, punchy anecdotes to back up an argument, rather than long stories.

It is about being appropriate for the audience, and appropriate for the speaker. Generally, speakers (particularly those who are not accomplished speakers) will find it easier to use shorter, punchier, fast-moving material, rather than getting bogged down in long stories.

Use of quotes

If a quote is relevant, appropriate and adds value, I will use a quote. It can be a bit like school: starting with a quote and finishing with a paradox. You end up looking a bit formulaic. The right quote at the right time can be absolutely incredible, but it certainly would not be part of the rule book.

Fear of public speaking

Glossophobia is considered to be people's number one fear. I believe that the real fear is not fear of the audience, but fear of delivering bad content. I know there are some people who need therapy rather than speech writing, but, with ninety percent of the clients who call our company for the first time saying, 'I'm petrified', once they actually have content that they are confident in, they talk about how much they are looking forward to delivering it.

We need to move from a fear of public speaking to a fear of delivering poor content, where you are afraid of making a fool of yourself. Yes, there is a problem, but it is a much smaller problem than you are led to believe.

What people want

Some people come to me and say, 'Interview me, ask me questions, give me a script.' We then develop that, and they will probably recite it word for word.

Others give us a draft, and are sixty percent of the way there. We polish it, edit it and make it easy for them to deliver. Then there are those in the middle who keep bashing it to and fro and make the words theirs.

I like to have a fully scripted speech at some stage in the

process. It is only by having a fully scripted speech that you can see the links. I am not precious. If a client reads it word for word, you know it has not been absorbed. I would much rather they add their own touch.

Coping with nerves

People are fearful about a wide range of things, including the audience response and potential hecklers.

The first way to avoid nervousness is to prepare. Whether you are going to read, learn or deliver with or without notes, you need to actually dress-rehearse. Wear the clothes you are going to wear on the day, and use the microphone you are going to use on the day. Ideally, go to the room you are going to be in on the day and repeat the speech so many times that your fear of your perform-ance begins to disappear.

Once you are actually in the room, you are going to get that surge of adrenaline and feel a bit nervous, but you can prepare for this. If you think you are going to shake, the last thing you want is to be holding flapping bits of paper. If you think you are going to have a dry mouth, make sure that you have a glass of water at hand.

There are three major tips when it comes to delivering that tend to help with nerves.

The first tip is to breathe out, which sounds simple. As you walk up on stage, exhale. It helps a great deal.

Force yourself to look at your audience. You may get some reassurance from people looking back at you and nodding or smiling. The gut reaction to fear is to curl up. If we start looking down and getting introspective, then we will lose the audience. It is about trying to ensure that you smile, maintain eye contact and mimic the audience's behaviour.

Lastly, deliver with confidence – which means slowly, with

emphasis and with positive body language. It comes back to preparation.

Learning off by heart

The normal advice is to learn your speech off by heart, so that it looks as if you are ad-libbing. However, you have got more to lose by getting this wrong than you have to gain by getting it right. You may worry about it, and it is possible that you will look as if you are trying to remember what is coming next. It can happen with even the most polished performer – look at Ed Miliband in 2014. He spent weeks learning his speech, and ended up forgetting the most important part.

I have seen it at weddings. One friend gave a really wonderful speech. I went up afterwards and said, 'From a speech-writer – that was brilliant.' He replied, 'I can't believe that I forgot to mention my mum.' Why not have notes? Nobody belittles you for having notes.

Use notes in the right way. If you speak slowly enough, you can glance down for a few milliseconds. Check what is coming next. Look at your audience, and then deliver it.

The worst mistake in speech writing

The worst mistake when writing a speech is writing for the written word rather than the spoken word. They are totally different art forms. A speech is all about sound bites: short, punchy sentences. You need to leave room to breathe. Do not use too many adjectives, keep your emphasis in the right places and think about where an audience will react and pause.

A lot of the strength of a speech is in the white space where you let the audience absorb what you are saying before you carry on.

In writing, people make the mistake of thinking about oneself and not one's audience, and therefore not being relevant.

The worst mistake in speech delivery

The most common mistake, when delivering a speech, is speaking too quickly.

The analogy I use when chatting to clients is, 'Imagine a live TV show, with a live audience. You generally have someone with a big placard saying 'Laugh', 'Clap' or 'Sigh'. The speaker has to remember that it is only their voice and their body language that gives off those vibes.

If you speak too quickly and keep your head down, you will not get a response; it is about playing to the audience.

Best speeches

There are so many fabulous speeches.

In terms of pure writing, some of Kennedy's stuff was brilliant – the 'Man On The Moon' speech, in particular. He was not a great speaker, but he said some incredible things. He was a terribly nervous public speaker. He shook so much that had to hold his hands together when speaking.

Obama's 'Yes We Can' speech is one of the most beautifully written, most inspirational modern speeches I have ever heard.

'I Have A Dream' was clearly delivered in a phenomenally powerful and impressive way.

Interview with Peggy O'Regan, Speech and Drama Teacher

When speaking in public, try to pretend you are speaking to friends. Be spontaneous, and give your knowledge and yourself generously and happily. There should be a fusion of oneself and one's audience into one entity, a warm sharing of information with like minds. Fear is selfish and self-centred. Forget yourself – think instead of informing or sharing with friends. Enjoy the experience rather than worrying. Have confidence in your voice and language, and only talk on subjects that you are interested in. Speak with sensitivity, naturalness, accuracy and clarity.

We cannot reveal anything if we hold ourselves back from the audience. Fear is overcome by the joy of sharing, so enjoy yourself, love your audience and make them love you. Come to your audience laden with gifts, then reach out and draw them in. Do not just send out your voice. Create an experience for your audience.

Dress comfortably and appropriately. Relax beforehand: relax your muscles, especially around the throat. Yawning (in private) is splendid for the relaxation of the pharynx.

Do not let in any negative thoughts. There is often a split second in which you decide to embrace negativity, or keep it out. It is the same with all thought, and you can school yourself to reject negative impulses. They are soul-destroying, damaging and selfish. You should think only of your gifts, and sharing them with others. Be confident and stand comfortably, with your legs slightly apart for double the support.

It is all about the voice

Let your voice carry your body. Your facial expression – your eyes and your whole being – will respond to your expression of mind and thought through your voice. Your voice is you: it tells the whole world about you, the unique individual. You and your voice are synonymous.

People rarely use the microphone correctly; they will speak anywhere but into it. Where delivery is concerned, projection is tied up with pace. The person who shouts, and shouts too rapidly, just creates a blur. There will always be people with hearing problems, wherever you are. You need to project.

The voice should be supported by healthy organs of articulation – the pharynx, the soft and hard palates, tongue, teeth, lips and nose, and healthy lungs for good breath support. When speaking, breathe in noiselessly, deeply and discreetly before each sentence. The voice should be carried on the breath to the lips, and floated off to reach the members of the audience. There should be enough breath support to carry the voice, which will be coloured by the truth and sincerity of your thoughts. The voice can be broken down into 'pitch', 'pace', 'pause' and 'pressure'. All four elements are needed for a balanced and interesting delivery. However, they must be used with discretion.

Pitch

The pitch helps to colour the tone of your speech, and is determined by the content. The pitch makes your voice musical, yet overuse of pitch can reduce its impact. Your mind is then taken from the content to the movement of the voice. To gain flexibility in pitch, practise saying sentences in different pitches, without losing the ease or sensitivity of the voice.

Pace

The pace is important. Slow down – Irish people speak far too quickly. It takes time for the voice to carry. If you speak too quickly, people cannot absorb what you are saying. The words will then catch up with each other, and start to blur. Pace your speech according to the response of your audience. If you cannot see a response, it means you are talking at people, not to people.

Pause

A pause is not a stop, and it is not an empty space. It is an element of skilful speech. A rhetorical pause is very effective. A dramatic pause takes place before and/or after a particular word within a sentence. In that famous line from *Hamlet*, 'To be or not to be', actors will add a pause in different places. Where you decide to put the pause depends on your personality. Pausing has an immediate effect on your audience: if you pause in the right place, it can wake them up. A skilled speaker will carry the audience with him over the longest pause, giving them time to reflect and absorb what has been said.

Pressure

Pressure or emphasis must be used carefully. Pressure relates to the amount of volume you put into a word. It can lift a sentence, or change its meaning entirely. It has limited use in public speaking. If pressure is used too much, it can ruin your speech. A pause before or after a word can often work much better.

Body language

If you are talking to a group of people, you are absolutely

dependent on your voice to carry your message and your personality. How you use your eyes and your gestures is secondary to how you use your voice. The voice is the most important part of you. If you concentrate on the voice and on communicating, your body will follow suit, and you will draw people in.

Posture and facial expression are important. Your feet should be shoulder-width apart, and your body should not be stiff. Avoid constant movement. Stillness has its part to play in the impact you make. Be careful not to be repetitive in your gestures; it can become monotonous. Be observant of how you use your hands and arms, as some gestures can be over-worked.

Fear of public speaking

Everyone has nerves. Remember that your fear has no real power – it is only we, and no one outside us, who can make us afraid. Past failure should not be regarded as incompetence, but a valuable gathering of experience which enables us to walk more securely along the path of success. External events cannot hurt us, unless we ourselves use them to hurt us.

Relaxation

Look on your audience as you would a guest in your home. Be glad that they came to listen. Find one face, and imagine a conversation with him or her until you have settled down.

Make sure there is no tension in your body before you speak, as tension comes through in your voice. If you are tense, your voice is going to be tense.

Relax your body. Breathe deeply. Think of something calm and beautiful, and take your mind off what you are about to do.

Chapter Fourteen

SUCCESSFUL PITCHERS

The best thing about being a pitch coach is meeting so many inspirational people and hearing their stories and witnessing their pitches. They have such a 'can-do' attitude, which is probably the biggest thing they can bring to a pitch. The entrepreneurs interviewed in this chapter are just a glimpse of the fabulous people I have had the opportunity to coach on start-up and accelerator programmes all over Ireland. They provide us with great hope for the future of entrepreneurship, both in Ireland and beyond.

Interview with Eamon Keane, CEO of Xpreso

I met Eamon when I coached the finalists of Ireland's Best Young Entrepreneur 2014. He won. I subsequently interviewed him on my radio programme.

Xpreso solves the last-mile problem in e-commerce by delivering to people, not places. This 'software-as-a-service' (SaaS) offering allows courier companies to increase first-time delivery success by offering accurate arrival times to customers, and complementary redirection options to end-consumers.

How much investment have you secured?

As of June 2015, I have raised €850,000 from ACT venture capital, Delta Partners, Mastercard and Enterprise Ireland.

How did you find pitching when you started out?

I had bit of pitching practice during my PhD, but I was not that confident at off-the-cuff presentations.

And since then?

I have learned to practise and have slides prepared.

What do you include in your content?

Depending on the audience, we have around one slide per minute, which outlines the problem, solution, market, team and financials. If it is an introductory deck, we may leave out financials.

Do you get nervous?

Yes, when I am not prepared.

Do you enjoy pitching?

Not particularly, but I do like demonstrating our product.

How do you prepare?

Make a pitch deck that is tailored to the audience.

Do you memorise your pitch?

I am pretty well-rehearsed at this point. I do not prepare a script these days.

What is your method of presentation?

PowerPoint.

Does pitching get easier?

Yes, once you know the material.

Do you have any tips?

If you know your product and market well, this knowledge will shine through even if the delivery of your pitch is not perfect.

Interview with Gail Condon, Founder of Writing for Tiny

I met Gail on the New Frontiers Programme in DIT's Hothouse in 2014.

How long have you been in business?

We have been building it for two and a half years, but trading for eleven months.

Can you give a brief description of your business?

We make highly personalised children's books that discuss changes, worries and milestones in their lives.

Have you been successful in securing any investment to date?

Yes. We are a HPSU (high-potential start-up) client of Enterprise Ireland, and we have won investment through the Ireland's Best Young Entrepreneur competition in winning Cork City's Best Start-up and Best Young Entrepreneur. We also took part in New Frontiers and Trinity's LaunchBox, both of which provided investment.

How did you find pitching when you started out?

I found it incredibly nerve-wracking.

How has your pitch evolved from when you started out?

It is a lot more focused, as is the business.

What do you include in your pitch?

I include the problem, solution, market, team, future and testimonials.

What is the biggest investment pitch you've done?

The HPSU – the high-potential start-up.

How long did you prepare for this pitch?

We prepared with two-days' work, and then another two days were spent on the slides.

Were you happy with your pitch on the day?

I was relatively happy, yes. Who is ever totally happy?

What was the best pitch you have ever made?

It was probably my pitch for Cork City's Best Start-up.

What is the worst pitch you have made?

It was my AIB Start-Up Academy pitch – I really let myself down. It was my worst case of nerves. I had taken the advice of too many people, and was very unhappy with the result. I have since learnt to follow my instincts.

Do you get nervous pitching?

Yes, as you are facing the unknown. You and your business are being judged, so that is not easy.

Do you enjoy pitching?

I have never had a truly terrible experience. It is always positive, but I am also always relieved when it is over.

How do you prepare for a pitch?

I start with the slides (rogue, I know!) and work on the wording afterwards. Our slides are very representative of the brand and what we do, so they are crucial.

How do you remember a pitch?

My slides give me clues.

Do you learn it off by heart, or do you follow keywords?

I follow keywords, I could never do the exact same pitch twice.

Do you use slides? If so, is it Prezi, PowerPoint, Keynote?

I use PowerPoint.

Does pitching get any easier?

Yes, it does. My nerves are not as out-of-control these days. However, you still need some nerves to drive you on.

What tips would you give to anyone who has to pitch for investment?

Be clear, make sure that it matches your business plan and try to be yourself. You cannot please them all.

Interview with James McElroy, Co-founder of HouseMyDog.com

I met James on the New Frontiers Programme in DIT's Hothouse in 2015, and I interviewed him on my radio programme.

How long have you been in business?

We launched in March 2014.

Can you give a brief description of your business?

HouseMyDog is an online service that connects dog owners with vetted dog sitters in homes across Ireland and the UK. It is a bit like Airbnb, but for dogs.

Have you been successful in securing any investment to date?

To date, HouseMyDog has secured angel investment and funding from Enterprise Ireland

How did you find pitching when you started out?

I had to do a lot of pitching when I was in college, so I was comfortable with the idea of pitching when I started HouseMyDog. It is one of those things that, the more you do it, the more comfortable you feel in relation to how you talk, and your body language.

How has your pitch evolved from when you started out?

We often change our pitch slightly depending on who we are pitching to. Our pitch has its core, which remains the same so that we can have a uniform message as to what we do and our goals, but certain elements of it will change to cater for who we are pitching to.

What do you include in your pitch?

We try to keep our pitch relatively short. Again, it depends on who we are pitching to. For example, if I am pitching to a group of students, they will have no interest in our financials. We put a minimum amount of content on our slides, as I find that slides filled with too much information can become overwhelming. Areas like the problem and the solution are included in all our pitches.

What is the biggest investment pitch you have ever made?

Our biggest pitch was in January 2015 for the Hothouse New Frontiers Programme, though we have given pitches with far bigger financial rewards and in front of a higher number of people. This pitch was in front of five judges. It was at a time when HouseMyDog really needed a break in order for us to keep the website up and running, and for myself and my co-founder (who is also my brother) to stay motivated. We had pitched at a few events before this and nothing had come from them, so when we landed the Hothouse Programme, which comes with funding, mentoring and office space, we were delighted.

How long did you prepare for that pitch?

We prepared for about a week.

Were you happy with your pitch on the day?

No. We walked out and both said that it had gone dreadfully. I think we were being hard on ourselves, but some of the questions we were asked after the pitch had caught us off guard. The pitch was fine, but we have fine-tuned it a lot since then.

What was the best pitch you have ever made?

Strangely, some of the best pitches I have given have resulted in nothing, if it is for something like a competition or partnership. I always think that the gauge of a good pitch is when people ask questions afterwards. If people are asking questions, it means they have an interest in the idea, and are comfortable enough to ask about it.

What was the worst pitch you ever made?

The worst pitch was in the earlier stages of the company, so, over a year ago at this stage. Our pitch deck had a lot of graphics in it, and they did not work. I had to talk on the spot about things that were not showing up on the slides, which was annoying. It threw me off guard a bit. Needless to say there were no questions after that one.

Do you get nervous pitching?

Yes, even when you know exactly what you are saying, I still get slightly nervous just before I pitch. I think that standing in front of a group of people is quite unnatural, and it can be a bit daunting.

When I am actually pitching, though, I feel fine. It is just in the few moments before I am about to start that I get slightly nervous.

Do you enjoy pitching?

Yes. It is important to be able to tell people about your start-up, and to let them know what you are trying to achieve. In order for HouseMyDog to be where it is at the moment, we have had to pitch a lot. Great opportunities can come from pitching to the right people, and that is what I enjoy about it.

How do you prepare for a pitch?

We would know who it is we are pitching to, and then tailor our pitch deck to make it interesting for the people who have to listen to us. I find that this is what keeps it precise.

How do you remember a pitch?

By now it is just one of those things, like listening to a song over and over again. You get to know the lyrics. Timothy and I are so familiar with our pitch that we remember it easily.

Do you learn it off by heart, or follow keywords?

Keywords have always worked better for me.

Do you use slides? If so, is it Prezi, PowerPoint, Keynote?

I use PowerPoint.

Does pitching get any easier?

There are a lot of variables, like who you are pitching to and to how many people, but once you comfortably know the content, the delivery becomes easier.

What tips would you give to anyone who has to pitch for investment?

Keeping it to the point is important. Ten to fifteen minutes is enough, in my opinion. Trying to get your pitch to fit that time frame can be difficult, but I would recommend it. We have been to competitions where we were only allowed four slides, and one minute per slide. That is very tough, and we learnt a lot about refining the pitch from having to do that.

Interview with Sinéad Kenny, CEO of DiaNia Technologies

Sinéad set up the company in 2013. I met her on the New Frontiers Programme in Galway Mayo IT, which she completed in January 2014.

Did you secure funding?

DiaNia secured Competitive Start Fund (CSF) and Innovation Voucher support from Enterprise Ireland. DiaNia Technologies was selected for funding by the EU in the latest round of the Horizon 2020 SME Instrument, for our innovative technology.

DiaNia Technologies is a research-and-development company specialising in extrusion technologies for catheter-based medical devices. ExtruLub Technology, our minimum viable product, provides inbuilt low-friction surfaces on the inside and outside of a catheter, enabling physicians to reach anatomies with smaller vessels.

Can you tell us about your pitch?

Embarrassingly, our pitch is hugely different from the first one we presented with. This is probably as much a reflection of what we have learnt about our business as it is our approach to pitching. The major learnings for me were about communicating a crystal-clear message to your audience and personalising as much as possible and making use of emotional cues.

What do you include in your pitch?

We include the problem, solution, market, team and financials. However, as we want to 'keep our secret-sauce secret', the solution has to be described through the benefits it can bring to manufacturers, end users and patients. We have, as a result, spent a great deal of time sculpting this message.

Do you get nervous?

Yes and no. It depends on the audience, and what is at stake. I can become really nervous when I am addressing someone in my particular industry, and there is a risk that I could impact upon my reputation. I also get nervous when the discussion might be centred around areas I do not have a great deal of experience in.

Have you made many other pitches?

Yes. I have pitched between twenty-five and thirty times since New Frontiers.

What was your best pitch?

My best pitch was actually when I did not realise that I was doing a pitch. There was an investor from another industry in town, and I presented to him to get feedback. He is a very successful entrepreneur, and has raised large funding rounds in the past. I went through my presentation with him to get tips on how I could improve my pitch, and now we are in the process of moving into negotiations. You never know when or where you might get funding.

What was your worst pitch?

I went to a two-day 'pitchathon' in which interested investors and companies looking for funding listened to talks from experienced fundraisers. During those two days there was a 'speed-pitching' event. The day before that I had received what I thought were bad results, and my confidence was at a low. However, I learnt a very important lesson: never give up, as you do not know what could be around the next corner.

How do you prepare?

I practise, practise, practise. I usually book a meeting room and set up my presentation, visualise my audience and get a group of people together who do not know my product, but have pitched themselves in the past. I run through any areas I feel a little weak on prior to the meeting. I try to relax immediately before the meeting, and listen to music or the radio while travelling there.

I try to remember any suggestions for improvement from the audience (I always have a pen and paper at the ready) and to include these for the next presentation. However, it is also important to focus on any positives you can take away and use these for the next pitch.

Do you memorise your pitch?

I never learn a pitch off by heart, as I think this kills any emotion and enthusiasm, and you can get stuck if you are focusing on what the next sentence is going to be. I have a lot of images in my presentations, and I use these as cues.

Does it get easier?

Absolutely.

Do you have any tips?

Talk to people who have pitched in the past and, if they are willing, do your presentation for them.

Be enthusiastic. More often than not, the investor is looking to invest in a person, not the product.

Be confident. It is easier said than done, but try to concentrate on the positives you got out of the last presentation, and think about the reasons the people around you support you and believe in you.

Be honest.

Always remember that you know the most about your product or business.

Interview with Olive O'Connor, Founder of MediStori

Olive O'Connor's business is Minimate Limited, which trades as MediStori. Olive set up her business in 2012. I met her on the New Frontiers Programme in Galway-Mayo IT, which she completed in January 2013.

MediStori provides self-management services and toolkits to the public, private and not-for-profit healthcare sectors. The first of these products is a personal health organiser called the MediStori. Since the New Frontiers Programme, Olive has been successful in securing investment.

Could you tell us about the pitch itself?

At first I tried to fit everything into one pitch to suit everyone, but now I know to concentrate on the audience in front of me. I do a lot of primary and secondary research, and then tap into some of what I would call the 'pains', so that they can get a better understanding of how our company's service or product could work in their own lives. As well as this, I now also address known barriers that I can foresee being asked after the pitch.

Could you tell us about your pitch content?

I never include financials, although I do include a business case, if necessary. I have a back-up slide just after the finishing piece that I use if I am asked about financials. I first talk about the high-level problem, and show the audience a glimpse of the solution in an elevator-pitch style. I then bring it back to me, and talk about my background, my problems and how the solution was developed. I then talk about the solution in more detail, including the benefits, risks, target market and the 'hows, whys and whats'. I then discuss the strategy of how I will deliver the service. I always end by explaining how my solution could help the world and the investor.

Is there an emotional element in the pitch?

I include an emotional element in my pitch. I used to get nervous about doing so when pitching to 'business' people, as I felt that it could be used against me. My product was designed out of need – my children, my husband and myself all have health issues, which was how I thought about creating a personal health organiser. I was nervous talking about our health issues, as I felt that judges would look upon this as me potentially not being able to run a business. So I lightened this by adding some jokes into the pitch. Emotions are so important in every pitch, be they sad, happy or funny – you have got to engage your audience.

Do you get nervous?

Yes! Very much so. But nerves are good – and I address these at the beginning of the pitch. If they are particularly bad – I usually say something funny to make the audience laugh, which calms me down.

Do you enjoy pitching?

I do now, but only because I go in with the attitude of not winning, but building relationships with people who could provide potential future investment.

Have you made many pitches?

I have not pitched for money, but I have presented at the international level to my customers and end-users. It is the same thing, really, except that you are not pitching for money but for buy-in from the audience. This can actually be harder.

What was your best pitch?

I did a very short three-minute pitch at the World Health Organisation VdGM forum. This was excellent, as I was presenting to GPs and really had to research their needs before I could get up there. I got such a great round of applause and lots of feedback – I was honestly gobsmacked with the response.

What was your worst pitch?

The worst pitch was my first one. I was too focused on trying to fit in everything I 'should' say as opposed to being myself. I was too stiff, and I realise now that it is okay not to say everything, as people will ask questions afterwards.

How do you prepare for a pitch?

I do my homework on the audience, and put in the hours to prepare my PowerPoint slides. I am creative by nature and so I get lost in the world of designing slides, but the benefit of doing this is that every time I go over them it drills home to me the information that I am presenting. I also ask people to listen to me and check over everything I am saying, to get constructive feedback.

How do you remember a pitch?

I know my stuff inside and out. I use slides to guide me (these do not have text – they are visuals) and I also rehearse, rehearse, rehearse.

Do you learn it off by heart, or use keywords?

I never follow anything by heart – it is all about keywords and visuals – I cannot even learn the words of songs. I talk like I am telling a story.

Does pitching get any easier?

Yes it does, absolutely, get easier, but the research behind it does not. You still have to apply the same energy into doing your homework.

Do you have any pitching advice?

Do not lie or twist the truth. If everything you are saying is true, you cannot be caught out. Be honest, also, in that you should not be afraid to say that you are nervous. Take a few deep breaths before you go out there and smile. It can help if you focus on a point in the room when talking.

Try to get a feel for your investors' backgrounds, and what they are interested in. Make what you are doing relevant for them. Even try looking for something in the news. Do not presume that people know the 'lingo' you are using – keep everything clear and simple. Remember that even if they do not invest in you now, they may do so down the road.

Interview with Andrew MacFarlane, CEO of CareZapp

CareZapp has been in business since 2014. I met Andrew on the Bank of Ireland Accelerator Programme, which he completed in January 2015.

If you are receiving care or helping to care for someone at home, chances are you could use a hand. CareZapp has a simple way of connecting those who care. CareZapp connects family, the care community and technology to best enable and support a loved one at home. Andrew has been successful in raising Competitive Start Funding (CSF) through Enterprise Ireland. He received €50,000, in addition to €25,000 in founder and accelerator investment.

How has your pitch evolved from when you started out?

I had quite a bit of experience presenting to an audience on topics and business in the past, but I still found pitching to be a difficult and stressful experience. My pitch has evolved a lot from when it started out. I now focus more on a telling a story. I have removed a lot of fluff and unnecessary complexity, and focus instead on what simple message I want that particular audience to hear.

What content do you include in your pitch?

One pitch does not suit them all – you need to tailor it according to the interests and criteria of your audience – but most areas are still covered, particularly the problem, solution, the market, the team and the question 'why now?'

Can you tell us about TechCrunch UK?

CareZapp was accepted onto TechCrunch UK in November 2014. TechCrunch Disrupt is one of the most anticipated annual technology conferences, and is hosted by TechCrunch in San Francisco, New York City, London and elsewhere. It is typically where technology start-ups seek to launch their products and services. It is highly competitive, with some 800 companies competing for the event that we attended. Only fourteen companies got through, by competing onstage in front of venture-capital potential investors, media and other interested parties for prize money and publicity.

Was it a big deal?

It was an audience of up to 2,000 people, with hundreds of thousands checking in worldwide via webcam, and publicity that is syndicated around the globe. For a start-up, you would want to have very deep, deep pockets to match the publicity.

How did you prepare?

We had six to eight weeks of preparing for the event, and travelling to London a number of times to meet the TechCrunch team.

Were you happy with your pitch on the day?

Are you ever happy with your own pitch? I know there are things that could have been clearer, but yes, at the end of the day, as a team, we were delighted. We had lots of positive feedback and, of course, the TechCrunch write-up, video and images that still are important marketing collateral for us today.

Did you get investment from TechCrunch?

We got significant exposure that still brings people, companies and investors into the pipeline today. This was one of the factors in raising Competitive Start Funding. We have a number of high-profile funders tracking us, and we are currently in discussions on funding for a seed round.

What was your best pitch?

Our best pitches are any that end in a sale or a deal.

What was your worst pitch?

The worst pitches are when I have not done any research on my audience.

Do you ever nervous when pitching?

I am still nervous when pitching. A tip that another Irish entre-preneur from a previous TechCrunch gave me, which I still use for some events, was: pick your favourite uplifting music, and take the time to stop and listen to it just before pitching.

Do you enjoy pitching?

I cannot say that pitching is my favourite part of my role, but I do love pitching to people where we can bring a huge benefit with our product.

How do you prepare before a pitch?

I strive to understand my audience, and what takeaway message I want to get across to them.

How do you remember a pitch?

I use key blocks or pointers, and usually picture the keyword in my head.

Does pitching get easier?

No, not really. With practise, though, you can approach it in a way that is more focused on the desired outcome rather than the process of pitching.

What tips would you give to someone who has to pitch for investment?

Research the people you are pitching to, what previous investments they have made, whether they have made any in your area, what level they invest in.

Having a pitch coach available to us during and outside the accelerator made a huge difference. The fact that she had a huge amount of empathy with our target market also really helped – thank you, Catherine.

Chapter Fifteen

CATHERINE'S TOP TEN PITCH TIPS

1. The starting point of any pitch, presentation or speech is your audience. Research your audience. Who are they? Why should they care? How are they going to benefit? Find an emotional connection between you and your audience.

2. Structure your pitch, presentation or speech in a story format with a wow opening, three to five main points, a closing which includes a summary, an overlap with your opening, a thank you and an action or focus for the future.

3. Ensure that there is a logical link between your points. Take the audience by the hand, step by step, through your speech, pitch or presentation.

4. Keep your pitch, presentation or speech as concise, clear and simple as possible. Let there be no room for confusion.

5. Engage and entertain your audience with relevant examples and anecdotes that they will remember.

6. Vary the pitch and pace of your voice. Use pause and emphasis.

7. Ensure that you have a confident posture, with your shoulders back and your feet fixed to the floor. Keep your hands by your sides, and gesture normally. Use eye contact and maintain a pleasant facial expression.

8. Nerves are normal – just learn to manage them. Breathe mindfully, use visualisation and/or positive affirmations. Shift the focus from yourself to getting the message across to your audience. Change the spotlight on you to a floodlight on the audience.

9. Practise your pitch, presentation or speech as often as possible. Speak from the heart.

10. Be interested and passionate about the topic of your speech, pitch or presentation. It will have a ripple effect on your audience.

★

One final takeaway message:
    Be yourself.
    Be the best of yourself.
    Have no fear.
    Allow yourself to shine.